INFLUENZA
The Next Pandemic?

INFLUENZA
The Next Pandemic?

CONNIE GOLDSMITH

Twenty-First Century Medical Library

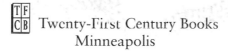

Twenty-First Century Books
Minneapolis

The images in this book are used with the permission of: Centers for Disease Control and Prevention Public Health Library (CDC)/Dr. Erskine Palmer, pp. 2, 7, 12, 14 (top left), 21, 39, 49, 62, 72, 90; CDC, pp. 14 (bottom left), 64; CDC/Frederick A. Murphy, p. 14 (right); © Shehzad Noorani/Peter Arnold Inc., p. 18; © Bettmann/Corbis, pp. 23, 51; © Hulton Archive/Getty Images, p. 24; National Archives (W&C 439), p. 27; Library of Congress, pp. 29 (LC-USZ62-108266), 31 (LC-USZ62-126995); CDC/Laura Westlund, p. 35; AP/Wide World Photos, pp. 41, 53, 54, 91; © Gary Lau/Next Photo/CORBIS SYGMA, p. 77; © Frederic J. Brown/AFP/Getty Images, p. 83; CDC/Courtesy of Cynthia Goldsmith, Jacqueline Katz, and Sharif R. Zaki, p. 86; CDC/James Gathany, p. 92; © STR/AFP/Getty Images, p. 94.

Cover: CDC/Dr. Erskine Palmer; CDC/Jim Gathany (inset).

Special thanks to my writing partners, Erin Dealey, Patricia M. Newman, and Laura Torres, for their endless support and encouragement, and to microbiologist Ken S. Rosenthal, Ph.D., for his valuable assistance

Twenty-First Century Books
A division of Lerner Publishing Group
241 First Avenue North
Minneapolis, MN 55401 U.S.A.

Website address: www.lernerbooks.com

Library of Congress Cataloging-in-Publication Data

Goldsmith, Connie, 1945–
    Influenza : the next pandemic? / by Connie Goldsmith.
      p.   cm. — (Twenty-first century medical library)
    Includes bibliographical references and index.
    ISBN-13: 978-0-7613-9457-0 (lib. bdg. : alk. paper)
    ISBN-10: 0-7613-9457-5 (lib. bdg. : alk. paper)
    1. Influenza. 2. Influenza—History. I. Title. II. Series.
RA644.I6G65 2007
614.5'18—dc22   2005023588

Manufactured in the United States of America
1 2 3 4 5 6 – BP – 12 11 10 09 08 07

CONTENTS

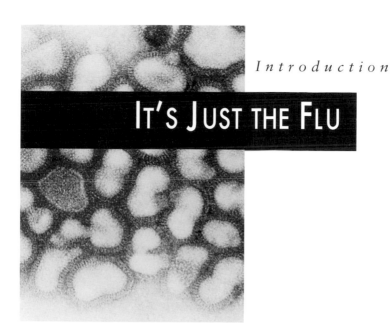

IT'S JUST THE FLU

Emily, Fifteen

Emily is interested in genealogy—studying her family's history. Right now she's researching her great-uncle Johnny who died in 1918 during World War I (1914–1918). Her grandmother just gave her a bunch of very old letters. Emily was surprised to discover that her great-uncle didn't die of war injuries; in fact, he never even left the United States.

Jake, Sixteen

Jake has a lot going on in his life. First, there's the basketball game on Friday night—it's the regional semifinals. Then he's going to a big party with his girlfriend, Trish. Jake also promised his dad that he'd hit a bucket of golf balls with him at the driving range on Saturday. And sometime on Sunday, he has to find a couple of hours to study for a history test.

Daveon, Fifteen

Daveon has had asthma since he was five years old. He tries hard to remember to use his inhalers as his doctor tells him to, but sometimes he forgets. Daveon has to take a breathing treatment at home every night just before bedtime. Even though he does everything right, asthma remains a big problem for Daveon, and he's sick of it.

Ben, Thirteen

Ben's grandma Rose lives with him and his mom. Rose is sixty-eight and has diabetes. Ben worries about his grandmother a lot because she doesn't take very good care of herself. Ben sometimes catches her smoking in the backyard, even though the doctor told her to stop after she got pneumonia last year.

Linh, Fourteen

Linh lives in the Vietnamese countryside where her family raises chickens and ducks for the food markets in Ho Chi Minh City. Before school each morning, Linh and her seven-year-old brother, Loc, feed the birds and gather eggs. In the evenings, it's Loc's job to catch a chicken for dinner, while Linh helps her mother prepare it for the evening meal.

Influenza will affect all of these young people or their families, just as it may affect you and your family. Maybe you've had the flu (a shortened form of the word *influenza*) or seen your school closed down because of an outbreak. Maybe you had to look after your little brother or cook dinner for a few days because your mom was too sick to do it. Or maybe one of your grandparents died of the flu or its complications.

"It's just the flu," people say, but getting the flu is nothing to sneeze at. The aches and pains, high fever, headache, cough, and lingering weakness can knock you off your feet for a couple of weeks. It may take close to a month to recover from the severe fatigue that flu leaves behind as an unwanted souvenir for its sufferers.

Flu is a serious problem for everyone. Each year it infects up to 20 percent of Americans, puts 200,000 of them into the hospital with flu-related complications, and kills about 36,000. The cost of treating flu, including lost wages and productivity of sick workers, is billions of dollars each year in the United States alone. The World Health Organization (WHO) estimates that worldwide, between 3 and 5 million people each year get bad cases of flu. Between 250,000 and 500,000 people die of the flu every year. Tens of millions more get milder cases.

The word *influenza* comes from the Italian word *influentia*, because people used to believe that the influence of the planets, stars, and moon caused the flu. Today we know that the flu isn't caused by any of these things. We know that some really nasty viruses are the culprits. Scientists believe that flu viruses moved from waterfowl, such as ducks and geese, into humans and other mammals thousands of years ago.

Which would you choose as the cause of the single deadliest epidemic in history—plague, smallpox, AIDS, or flu? The plague killed an estimated one-third of the entire population of medieval Europe in four or five years. Smallpox terrorized the planet for twelve thousand years. And AIDS has killed about 20 million people since scientists first identified the HIV virus in 1983. In spite of the huge death tolls exacted by these terrible diseases, the correct answer is that the flu is the most deadly of the four. According to medical historians, the single deadliest epidemic in history occurred just as World War I drew to an end. During the winter of 1918–1919, a dangerous new strain of influenza swept around the world, ultimately killing between 50 and 100 million people. The Spanish flu, as it's often called, killed more people in twenty-four weeks than AIDS did in twenty-four years. It killed more people in one year than smallpox or the Black Plague did in fifty years.

When Spanish flu struck the world, people were focused on the hardships of wartime. Many countries, including the United States, censored the press during the war. No country wanted the enemy to know that tens of thousands of its soldiers were sick! So the flu received limited newspaper coverage, and few people at the time had any idea of its worldwide impact. Mostly, people only knew what was going on in their own communities. The Spanish flu faded into memory. Instead, history books were filled with stories about how the war started, how it was fought, and how it ended.

A few smaller epidemics over the past fifty years set off alarm bells in researchers' minds, triggering them to search for the cause of the Spanish flu. They wonder if that strain of flu could ever come back. There's no answer yet, but the science of genetics is providing clues about why that epidemic was so very deadly. And it's important to get an answer soon.

Today a new strain of flu has emerged, and world health officials are warning that it may well become the next killer pandemic. Called bird flu or avian flu, the strain is unique in that it passes directly from birds to people. Normally, flu passes from birds to mammals—usually pigs—and then to humans. Bird flu appears to be even more deadly to humans than the Spanish flu.

The only thing that holds bird flu in check for now is that it isn't easily passed between people. However, doctors worry that a person who is sick with one of the usual strains of human flu might become infected with bird flu at the same time. If that happens, the two viruses could mutate or recombine to produce a highly contagious and deadly new disease. The frightening news about bird flu has pushed politicians and health officials to start preparations for a possible epidemic. The rush is on to stock up on antiflu medications and to complete the development and testing of a vaccine for bird flu.

This book provides information about flu, how it spreads, and how it is prevented and treated. The chapters will also discuss past flu epidemics, the next potential epidemic of bird flu, as well as promising new research. Turn to the next chapter to learn how the tricky shape shifters known as flu viruses make us so sick.

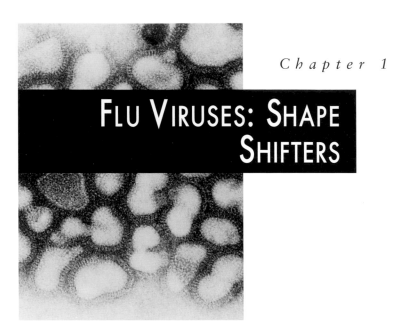

FLU VIRUSES: SHAPE SHIFTERS

Not really alive, yet not quite dead, viruses are the zombies of the microscopic world. They don't carry on any of the activities that define life. Viruses can't move or reproduce by themselves. They don't need water, food, or even oxygen to survive. In fact, they can't do anything at all until they get inside a living cell. Viruses live in a state of suspended animation until they find just the right host organism, whether it be plant, bird, animal, or human.

Viruses have been around a very long time. Virologists, scientists who study viruses, are not certain where viruses came from, but they have three theories. Some virologists believe that viruses started as living cells and devolved into simpler organisms, unlike most life, which evolves into more complex forms. Another theory is that viruses originated as primitive particles capable of replicating themselves. The third theory is that viruses were once parts of cells that broke away to evolve separately. Regardless of their origin, viruses don't seem to serve any useful purpose at all, unlike bacteria or fungi, some of which are necessary for life.

Without living cells to infect, most viruses survive only a few hours. But there is plenty of life for a virus to choose from—plants, birds, animals, and people. And once inside a living organism, viruses are easily transmitted. They can enter our body through breaks in the skin and by way of mucous membranes of the mouth, nose, and genitals.

For example, the virus that causes AIDS is passed by sexual contact or by dirty needles shared by drug users. People get hantavirus when they breathe in tiny, powdered particles of urine and feces left by infected mice. Mosquitoes transmit West Nile virus when they bite people. And people who are sick with the flu spew out millions of viruses every time they cough or sneeze.

SMALLER THAN SMALL

Viruses are between twenty and one hundred times smaller than bacteria and can only be seen through an electron microscope. Viruses are so tiny that millions of them could fit inside the period at the end of this sentence. A chicken pox virus is 0.000005 inch (0.0001 millimeters) long, while a polio virus is even smaller at 0.000001 inch (0.00003 millimeters). Though tiny, viruses come in shapes as different as fluffy cotton balls, bulletlike cylinders, and handless rolling pins. Some viruses appear as bristled balls that have so many spikes they resemble floating antiship mines.

Viruses are also much simpler than bacteria. They are inert bundles of genetic material in search of a host. The outer shell of a virus may be a protein shell called a capsid, or it may be a fatty membrane called an envelope, which is made up of lipids and proteins. Viruses use several forms of genetic material—double-stranded DNA (deoxyribonucleic acid) or RNA (ribonucleic acid), or single-stranded DNA or RNA. The influenza virus contains eight segments of RNA, which carry its genetic information.

Most viruses have external protrusions, which allow them to dock with and then invade the host organism. These projections are made of protein and also act as antigens—substances that activate the host's immune system. These protruding antigens determine which kinds of living cells a virus will attach to and enter. For example,

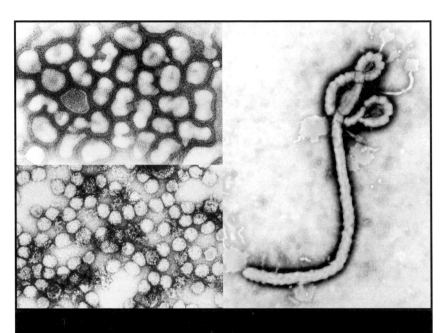

Viruses exist in many shapes and sizes. The globular shaped viruses *(top left)* are influenza A viruses, the type of flu with the potential to cause sweeping epidemics. The yellow fever virus *(bottom left)* is spherical. The Ebola virus *(right)* has a distinct hooked shape and causes a lethal hemorrhagic fever.

the flu virus is primarily interested in the cells that line the respiratory tract of birds and mammals.

The sole purpose of a virus is to get inside a cell and turn it into a factory to produce new viruses. The virus enters the cell like a tough supervisor carrying his own genetic coding on a blueprint. Once inside, he forces the host cell to provide the carpenters and electricians and bricklayers needed to build new viruses. Without workers to carry out the orders, the supervisor virus would be waiting outside, clutching the useless blueprint until it fell apart.

Viruses reproduce incredibly fast. While it takes about twenty years on average for humans to produce their next generation, viruses take only a tiny fraction of that time. Once viruses get inside a living cell and gain control of its reproductive machinery, some can churn out a new generation every two to three hours.

With such rapid reproduction comes a very high rate of mutation—a random and spontaneous change in the chemical structure of genes. Viruses mutate more in one day than humans did in several million years. Most genetic mutations are harmful to organisms, including viruses. But viruses have such a high rate of mutation that some of the changes may benefit the virus and help it adapt to its environment.

It's not just the rapid replication of new viruses that's responsible for so many mutations. Viruses cannot repair their mutations because they lack the necessary genetic tool kits. When a genetic mutation occurs in true life-forms, such as plants, animals, and humans, the cells often repair themselves before they reproduce. That way, new cells are undamaged by the mutation. It's like using spell-check on your computer to find and correct misspelled words before turning in your report. Viruses aren't big enough to carry around anything so complex as a genetic repair kit. This means mutations that don't kill the virus will be passed on to the next generation.

Another reason why viruses mutate so much is that some viruses exchange genes with one another as easily as kids swap hot new trading cards. When two viruses infect the same cell, they may splice together new combinations of genes or segments of genes, forming a new hybrid virus. This sharing and recombination of genes can result in dangerous new mutations that the human immune system may not be able to recognize or combat.

THE SHAPE-SHIFTING FLU VIRUS

Influenza viruses belong to the family of viruses called *Orthomyxoviridae*. The flu virus primarily infects birds and mammals, including humans. Flu viruses contain only eight strands of RNA. The viruses look round, somewhat like dandelions. About six hundred protein protuberances in two different shapes poke out from the virus's lipid envelope.

The first sort of protein protrusion is a pointed shape called hemagglutinin. Its specialty is binding to a cell. The spiky shape makes hemagglutinin the perfect device to latch onto the flu virus's favorite site in the human body, cells of the respiratory tract in the throat and lungs. Once the virus has successfully docked with a cell, more spikes of hemagglutinin latch on like so many grappling hooks. Finally, the virus enters the host cell where it dumps its RNA. The genetic material hijacks the cell's reproductive machinery and forces it to make thousands of daughter viruses.

Meanwhile, the second kind of antigen, called neuraminidase, specializes in helping to spread the infection from cell to cell. Viewed under an electron microscope, neuraminidase has a boxy head at the end of a stalk. The head is crowned with what looks like four six-bladed propellers. These propeller-like devices are actually enzymes that destroy protective chemicals on the cell's surface. This allows the daughter viruses to escape from host cells and spread to other cells. From the time the flu virus attaches to a cell, it takes about ten hours for these daughter viruses—between one thousand and ten thousand of them—to exit the original cell and move on to invade and infect other cells.

Like all viruses, flu viruses are continually mutating. When a flu virus mutates, it usually causes only slight changes in the hemagglutinin and neuraminidase. But that happens often enough to enable the virus to escape detection by the immune system. If the immune system can't "see" the virus, it can't fight it.

Imagine two football teams on a field. Viruses make up the offensive team. They're wearing gold pants and blue shirts. Say the referee (the immune system) wants to call a penalty on the virus players. At first, it's easy for the referee/immune system to identify the offensive virus players because their uniforms are different from the other team (maybe the defensive team is wearing red and white).

If the virus players add a stripe to their gold pants, the referee/immune system would still be able to recognize them. But if the virus players switch to blue pants and gold shirts, the immune system would have more trouble figuring out who was who. The freshly mutated hemagglutinin and neuraminidase are like new uniforms, but underneath them, most of the football players' bodies (the viral RNA) remain much the same.

Scientists have named the flu virus's shape-shifting powers. Relatively minor and gradual change to the hemagglutinin and neuraminidase is called *antigen drift*. Antigen drift is slow but continual and is responsible for outbreaks of flu and smaller epidemics.

Every ten to twenty years, the viral genetic changes are so sudden and so radical that nobody's immune system can identify the new virus. This is called *antigen shift*. Think of the football team again. Antigen shift would occur if the players completely changed their uniforms, moving from gold pants and blue shirts to green pants and black shirts. The referee/immune system wouldn't have a chance of recognizing the offensive team (the flu virus) hidden inside their new uniforms.

The shape-shifting flu virus has another trick. One cell can be infected by two different flu viruses. The viruses can even come from different animals, such as a pig and a bird. When that happens, both sets of RNA are inside the cell. The viruses can re-assort (mix) segments of RNA, creating a new

17

virus. If the human immune system doesn't recognize the new virus, it cannot fight it. Antigen shift is responsible for big epidemics and worldwide infections called pandemics.

Viruses cause a lot of diseases, including mumps, measles, and polio. You probably don't remember being vaccinated against those diseases when you were a little kid. Once people have been vaccinated against mumps, measles, or polio, they can't get the disease. However, flu viruses change so much faster than other viruses that scientists must make a new vaccine against them every year. That means people who want to be immunized against the flu (more about that in chapter 4) must get vaccinated each year in order to be protected against the newest strain.

HOME SWEET HOME

Scientists believe that most flu outbreaks originate in densely populated areas of China where conditions are just right. Flu viruses are a little picky about where they make

This family in Asia lives closely with the poultry it keeps. These conditions increase the likelihood of avian influenza viruses adapting to infect humans.

18

their home. They like a place where people, birds, and pigs live close together, preferably next to a pond or rice paddy. In this ideal home, wild migrating ducks, geese, gulls, and other water birds stop overnight. Maybe the wild birds are looking for a little company, a free handout of grain, or maybe they like the looks of the water. Whatever the reason, the wild birds mix it up with the locals.

All flu strains have been found in wild waterfowl and in the water where they live and fly over. In birds the flu virus lives primarily in the intestinal tract rather than in the respiratory tract, as with humans and other mammals. The virus is excreted in bird droppings. As wild water birds fly around the world, their virus-laced droppings fall into ponds, lakes, and even the ocean.

In most cases, the flu viruses don't make wild birds sick, which tells scientists that they've adapted to the viruses very well. However, domestic chickens, ducks, and geese can easily pick up the flu virus when they drink water contaminated by droppings from the wild birds. The domestic birds haven't adapted to the flu virus at all. They get very sick, and huge numbers of them die.

The flu virus also likes to have pigs living right next to the pond, drinking the flu-infected water and mingling with the birds. And on cold nights, the flu virus likes it best of all when the farmer brings those pigs into the house to curl up with the family. In China, pigs serve as living mixing bowls for flu viruses, providing a place where bird viruses can easily swap genes with pig viruses, before moving on to humans. China has the world's largest pig population and one-fifth of the world's human population. Virologist Kennedy Shortridge calls South China, "a virtual virus soup."

KNOW YOUR ABCs

Scientists have identified three types of flu: A, B, and C. Type A is the most common and the most dangerous. It infects a wide variety of birds, animals, and people. Birds, pigs, tigers, horses, and even whales and seals can get Type A flu. Type B only infects humans; it usually produces a milder illness than Type A flu. Type C flu is very mild and also only infects humans. The symptoms are so similar to the common cold that people seldom seek treatment for Type C flu.

Type A flu is divided into subtypes on the basis of its two antigens, hemagglutinin (H) and neuraminidase (N). There are 16 subtypes of H antigens and 9 subtypes of N antigens, producing a total of 144 different Type A flu viruses. Types B and C are not subdivided by their antigens. Type A and B flu strains are named according to where they first caused illness or for the species in which they were first identified. If the flu strain is Type A, it's then broken down further into subcategories according to which form of H and N it carries. Type C is not named.

For example, in 1957 a flu epidemic was caused by the A/Asian/H2N2 virus. This means that the virus was Type A, that it was first discovered in Asia, and that it carried subtype 2 of hemagglutinin and subtype 2 of neuraminidase. Usually several flu viruses are circulating at the same time. The viruses identified during the flu season of 2005–2006 were A/California/H3N2, A/New Caledonia/H1N1, and B/Yamagata. These are among the most common strains circulating today.

Scientists now know that the virus H1N1 caused the Spanish flu of 1918–1919, the worst pandemic in history. When medical historians looked at old farm records, they found thousands of pigs had been sick with runny noses and coughs at the same time people started getting sick. For years, scientists believed the people had been infected by the pigs. But in 2005, researchers discovered that the H1N1 flu that hit pigs and people at the same time in 1918 came from birds. In light of the current threat of a bird flu pandemic, this is troubling information. Turn to the next chapter to see how this flu spread from a handful of American farms to infect and kill millions of people around the world.

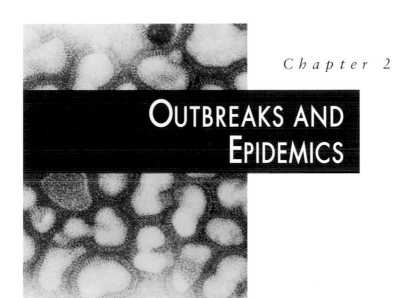

Chapter 2

OUTBREAKS AND EPIDEMICS

Emily's Story

Emily has been studying genealogy since she did a report about her family history in grade school. She's found out everything about her parents, aunts, uncles, and grandparents—when they were born, married, had children, and died. Now she's trying to find out about a great-uncle named Johnny Barnes. All she knew about him is that he was born in Illinois and that he died in 1918 during World War I.

Emily recently got a stack of old letters from her grandmother and was surprised to discover Johnny Barnes didn't die of a war injury. In fact, he never left the country. She deciphers the old faded handwriting of a letter written to Johnny's mother, Alice Barnes, her great-grandmother's sister.

21

The letter is from the commanding officer of an army camp in Georgia, telling Mrs. Barnes that her son had died of what was later called the Spanish flu. He was only twenty! Emily hopes that a kind nurse was with him and that he hadn't died alone. She had the flu herself last year and got over it in a week. She wonders how such a young man could have died of the flu.

The Spanish flu wasn't the first known flu pandemic. Influenza has been making people sick for about five thousand years. Scientists believe that centuries ago, the flu virus mutated in central Asia, allowing it to move from birds into animals and humans. In 412 B.C., the Greek physician Hippocrates, often called the father of medicine, wrote about what was likely influenza. Although flu is a highly contagious disease, travel was slow during ancient times. People journeyed on foot, on the backs of camels and horses, or by small boats. If flu broke out in isolated villages, it was unlikely to spread very far.

By the 1500s, people were sailing around the world in large ships. Flu, like bubonic plague and smallpox, could easily be passed by sailors as ships traveled from port to port. Sketchy records suggest several flu epidemics occurred in Europe that century. An outbreak spread from Europe into Africa and Asia in 1580, making it the first known pandemic. A major pandemic from 1889–1890, named the Russian flu because it spread from Russia and Asia eastward to Europe, was the deadliest-known flu pandemic of history up to that point.

In 1892, after the Russian flu pandemic was over, German bacteriologist Richard Pfeiffer reported that he had discovered the cause of flu. Using a microscope, he examined mucous from flu victims and found large numbers of a new bacteria. He named it after himself, Pfeiffer's Bacillus. Today we know that bacterial infections, including those caused by Pfeiffer's Bacillus, commonly follow flu.

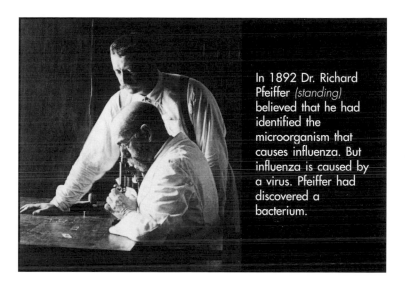

In 1892 Dr. Richard Pfeiffer *(standing)* believed that he had identified the microorganism that causes influenza. But influenza is caused by a virus. Pfeiffer had discovered a bacterium.

While the bacteria Pfeiffer identified now bears the name *Haemophilus influenzae*, it is not that bacteria but a virus that causes influenza. And it was a flu virus that caused the greatest pandemic in human history.

A PERFECT STORM

A perfect storm—the coming together of conditions favorable for a calamitous event, can happen on land as well as at sea. Severe overcrowding, outbreaks of disease, and huge numbers of cold and poorly clothed men on the move are the conditions that conspired to create the perfect storm of what came to be called the Spanish flu pandemic of 1918–1919.

The hardships of World War I provided the gathering clouds of catastrophe. Europe had been at war for three years by the time the United States declared war on Germany in April 1917. By the end of June, ten million young American men had signed up for the military. The U.S. government quickly set up dozens of training camps around the nation.

Medical staff attend to Spanish flu sufferers at a tent hospital near Lawrence, Kansas, in 1918. Some medical historians believe the Spanish flu started in Kansas.

Within months some camps had ten thousand or more recruits crowded into quarters meant for half that number.

The winter of 1917–1918 was unusually cold. Heating fuel and heavy clothing was in short supply. The army couldn't keep the men warm enough. Military camps suffered outbreaks of measles and pneumonia that left the soldiers weakened and susceptible to the flu that would strike a few months later. Even when sick, men were stuffed into trains and shipped from small camps to larger ones. Then they were shuffled off to port camps along the eastern seaboard and onto ships headed for the European battlefields.

Today's medical historians have traced the likely beginning of the Spanish flu, and it didn't come from Spain. Many suspect that a new flu virus originated in Haskell County, Kansas, late in 1917 or early in 1918. The county's tiny towns lay west of Dodge City in rich farmland dense with hogs and chickens, conditions ripe for the emergence of a new flu virus. During January and February of 1918, a country doctor named Loring Miner realized that the flu raging through his county was violent and unlike any that he'd ever witnessed. Unlike today, influenza was not a reportable disease; however, this strain seemed so unusual that Dr. Miner reported it to the U.S. Public Health Service.

Between February 28 and March 2, three Haskell County boys named Dean Nilson, Ernest Elliot, and John Bottom shipped off to Camp Funston, Kansas (now Fort Riley), about 300 miles (483 kilometers) away. The huge training camp held fifty-six thousand men packed into chilly barracks and drafty tents. It's believed that one or more of the Haskell County recruits carried the mysterious virus along with him when reporting for duty at Camp Funston.

On March 4, 1918, a cook reported to sick call with the flu. That young private had what may have been the first case of Spanish flu in the military.

By the end of the month, thousands at the camp had fallen ill. Sick soldiers in transit carried the flu to Camps Forrest and Greenleaf in Georgia where one out of ten men fell ill. Other camps soon erupted with influenza. Out of the thirty-six largest military camps in the United States, twenty-four experienced flu outbreaks in the spring of 1918. Thirty of the fifty largest U.S. cities, many of them close to military bases, suffered flu outbreaks that same spring as well. But the worst was yet to come.

While the death toll was higher than usual for the flu, it wasn't high enough to really alarm health officials. That would happen some months later after troops had streamed from Camp Funston to other U.S. bases, and then on to European port cities. No one suspected that these young soldiers carried their own contribution to the killing fields of Europe.

THE NEXT WAVE

Like other epidemics, influenza outbreaks often come in waves. The next wave of the Spanish flu started in Brest, France. This port city in northwestern France was the place where most U.S. troops landed after reaching Europe.

Like a pebble tossed into a pond, the flu spread outward in ever-widening circles. Wherever soldiers gathered for sleep or meals or battle, the flu jumped from man to man. By the middle of April 1918, flu hit the French and Italian armies. British troops carried it from Brest to Great Britain in May. It reached Germany as well. German commander Erich von Ludendorff blamed the flu for keeping his troops from winning a major battle, a battle that might have turned the tide of war.

The flu soon reached Spain. Because Spain was neutral during the war, its newspapers were not censored. Reports of the flu filled Spanish papers, especially after Spain's ruler, King Alphonse XIII, fell seriously ill. Newspapers of the warring nations—the United States, France, England, Italy, Germany, and others—were censored. The papers weren't allowed to publish stories about the flu epidemic for fear of lowering military and public morale. Also, a story about thousands of sick soldiers might alert the enemy to a weakened fighting force. Since people around the world first read about the flu outbreak in connection with Spain, it became known forever—incorrectly—as the Spanish flu.

The flu quickly spread throughout Europe and Asia. It hit India in the middle of May 1918, carried to its ports by Allied transport ships. India's vast network of railroad lines carried flu deep into its interior regions. The flu spread to China, reaching Shanghai by the end of May, then swept over the rest of the world like a giant tsunami. It flooded into New Zealand, then over to Australia, where it sickened a third of the entire population.

Even though hundreds of thousands of troops fell ill from the flu in the spring and summer of 1918, it still wasn't as deadly as first feared. Soldiers called it the three-day fever. It made them pretty sick for a few days, but most made a good recovery. By the middle of August, it seemed as though the flu had disappeared. On August 10, 1918, British military authorities declared that the Spanish

New U.S. recruits pack a train headed for training camp and then fighting in Europe during World War I. Unknowingly, many were probably carrying the influenza virus.

flu epidemic had ended, and the country turned its attention back to the war. That was a bit optimistic.

The Spanish flu virus had only gone into temporary hiding, mutating and adapting itself. Today scientists know that viruses can become more dangerous as they pass from person to person, a process called passage. With each passage, a virus can become a better and more efficient killer.

Dr. Macfarlane Burnet, who shared the 1960 Nobel Prize in Medicine, estimated that the Spanish flu virus had undergone fifteen to twenty human passages after the relatively mild spring wave. The virus reemerged in the fall with a virulence never seen before. It was this second and most lethal wave that earned the Spanish flu the nickname, purple death.

PURPLE DEATH

Even as British authorities declared the epidemic over in August, it reemerged later that month as an even more dangerous disease. In Brest, France, where U.S. troops continued to disembark by the thousands, so many French soldiers flooded into the hospital that it had to turn away new patients. As French and U.S. soldiers left Brest, they carried the virulent new strain along with them. One ship carried it to Africa, hastening the worldwide spread of Spanish flu.

Freetown, in Sierra Leone, Africa, was a major coaling center for military ships traveling from Europe to South Africa and Asia. The British ship HMS *Mantua*, carrying 200 flu-stricken sailors, infected local workers in Freetown when it landed in mid-August. The dockworkers—those who survived—then infected the crew of every ship stopping to fill up with coal. Nearly 600 out of 779 crew members of the HMS *Africa* fell ill. When the transport ship HMS *Chepstow Castle* coaled at Freetown on its way from New Zealand to Europe, 900 out of a crew of 1,150 fell ill. Ships that had passed through Freetown delivered thousands of sick and dying soldiers to port cities around the world.

When the Spanish flu returned to the United States in its deadly new form, Americans feared the Germans had put "flu bacteria" into Bayer aspirin (which was manufactured in Germany at that time). Others believed that the Germans had sneaked into U.S. waters on U-boats and released the flu in Boston Harbor.

The Spanish flu hit Camp Devens, 35 miles (56 km) northwest of Boston, with a terrible vengeance. Already hard hit by outbreaks of measles and pneumonia, the overcrowded camp was unprepared for the flu. By September 22, 1918, one out of every five men at Camp Devens had the flu, and three-fourths of those with it were sick enough to be in the hospital.

Yet soldiers were still on the move, shuttling to camps around the nation, carrying the flu virus to both coasts and into the nation's midsection. On September 25 at Camp Grant, Illinois, 3,108 troops boarded a train headed to Camp Hancock, Georgia. By the time the train had chugged the 950 miles (1529 km) between the bases, it had become a death train. Almost every man on board had the flu. When the train reached its destination, 2,000 of the troops were hospitalized and dozens died.

From military camps, the Spanish flu quickly spread across the country and into the civilian population. Philadelphia was especially hard hit when the flu raced through the city after a huge war bond rally on September 28, 1918. Thousands of Boy Scouts, soldiers, sailors, and members of women's clubs marched in the 2-mile-long (3-km-long) parade to show their patriotism. Within three days, *every bed* in Philadelphia's thirty-one hospitals was filled with flu victims. In one emergency flu hospital, nearly a quarter of the patients died every day, only to be replaced by hundreds more the next day. Doctors and nurses died just as often as other people did, leaving few medical staff to care for the ill.

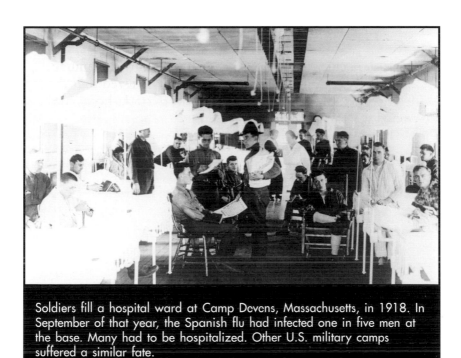

Soldiers fill a hospital ward at Camp Devens, Massachusetts, in 1918. In September of that year, the Spanish flu had infected one in five men at the base. Many had to be hospitalized. Other U.S. military camps suffered a similar fate.

LETTER FROM CAMP DEVENS

In 1959 a letter was found in a trunk of medical papers at the University of Michigan. The letter, dated September 29, 1918, was written by Dr. Roy Grist, a military doctor working at Camp Devens, Massachusetts. In the letter, addressed to one Dr. Burt, Dr. Grist describes the horror of the Spanish flu.

My Dear Burt:

Camp Devens has about 50,000 men, or did have before this epidemic broke loose. These men start with what appears to be an ordinary attack of la grippe or influenza, and when brought to the hospital, they very rapidly develop the most vicious type of pneumonia that has ever been seen.

Two hours after admission they have mahogany spots over the cheek bones, and a few hours later you can begin to see the cyanosis extending from their ears and spreading all over the face, until it is hard to distinguish the colored men from the white. It is only a matter of a few hours then until death comes and it is simply a struggle for air until they suffocate. It is horrible.

It takes special trains to carry away the dead. For several days there were no coffins and the bodies piled up something fierce. An extra long barracks has been vacated for the use of the morgue. It would make any man sit up and take notice to walk down the long lines of dead soldiers all dressed and laid out in double rows.

We have lost an outrageous number of nurses and doctors. It may be a long time before I can get another letter to you. My boss just gave me a lot more work to do, so I will have to close this. Good By old Pal. God be with you till we meet again.

Roy

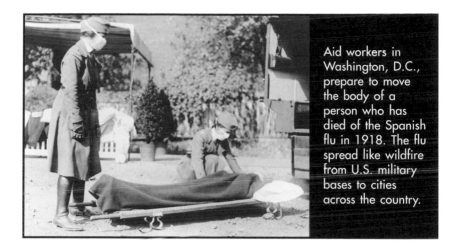

Aid workers in Washington, D.C., prepare to move the body of a person who has died of the Spanish flu in 1918. The flu spread like wildfire from U.S. military bases to cities across the country.

More than one-half million people got the flu in Philadelphia, and hundreds of people died *each day*. The dying lay neglected at home and were often just wrapped in a sheet and put in an empty room after death. Those who didn't get the flu lived in desperate terror for their lives, surrounded by the horror of their friends, family, and neighbors falling ill and dying. Everywhere, dead people were stacked like piles of wood because there was no one to bury them and all the coffins had already been used. Young children starved because adults were too sick to care for them or else they had died.

And that was just one U.S. city. The same horrific scene was repeated around the nation, in New York City, Boston, Des Moines, Albuquerque, Baltimore, Kansas City, and Detroit. In Chicago four out of ten flu victims died, and in Los Angeles, the health director closed every school, church, and theater. In Phoenix, Arizona, most of the dogs were killed in the mistaken belief they carried flu. Health officials closed down the town of Gunnison, Colorado, before anyone got sick. Armed guards patrolled every street and railroad to keep people out. It worked; the flu never reached Gunnison.

In other towns, shoppers could not enter stores. They had to shout their orders through windows. Coughing in public and shaking hands were outlawed. People who spat in the streets were arrested. Many cities required people to wear cloth masks over their faces when they went out in public in a useless attempt to stop the spread of flu. Much of the nation shut down, stayed indoors, and held its collective breath, hoping the flu would not find them.

No one had ever seen such a flu. Within hours, bloody fluid choked the lungs, making it impossible to provide oxygen to the body. A severe lack of oxygen can turn people the same color as the purple blue veins on the inside of the wrist. Doctors started calling the disease purple death. Some patients turned nearly black before they died, drowned in their own fluids. Blood poured from the lungs, noses, and ears. In the worst cases, people died in one or two days. The public feared that the Black Plague had reached America's shores, but it was "just the flu."

Throughout September, October, and November 1918, the flu surged west and south from the East Coast by water and rail, cresting in the largest cities, trickling down to the smallest towns and tiniest villages. By late November, it seemed as if the flu had burned itself out after this deadly second wave.

But the Spanish flu still hadn't finished with humanity. It returned in December 1918 after undergoing what is

A DEADLY RHYME

"I had a little bird and his name was Enza.
I opened the window and in flew Enza."

—*Nursery rhyme sung by American schoolchildren in 1918 and 1919* now known as antigenic drift—the lesser form of mutation. This third and final wave hit New York and San Francisco especially hard. Through the spring of 1919 and even into 1920, the Spanish flu stretched outward, spreading ever-smaller rivulets of infection.

AFTERMATH

Many pandemics, such as those caused by smallpox and plague, have changed the course of history. The Spanish flu is no exception. The Germans lost a vital battle due to high flu casualties among its soldiers. If they had won the battle, would they have won the war? U.S. president Woodrow Wilson, while attending peace talks in Paris, came down with a bad case of flu in April 1919. Some historians blame his lingering illness as the reason why he unexpectedly caved in to stringent French demands for the harsh peace terms that left Germany in economic shambles. Historians cite those harsh terms as a trigger leading to the rise of Adolf Hitler and World War II (1939–1945).

An estimated one-third of the world's population is believed to have fallen ill with the Spanish flu. Scientists today estimate the worldwide death toll at between 50 and 100 million. Compare that number to 280,000. That's how many people WHO estimated died in the 2004 tsunami disaster in Southeast Asia. At least another 100,000 people were missing and presumed dead. With the Spanish flu, like the tsunami, the exact number of dead will never be known. In the tsunami, untold numbers of people were swept out to sea and never recovered. With the flu, even larger numbers of people died at home or were buried in mass graves, often without ever being identified or even counted.

In the United States, the number of people who died of the flu is estimated to be 675,000, out of a 1919 population of 105 million. The Spanish flu killed more Americans in one year than the combined total who died in battle during World War I, World War II, the Korean War, and the Vietnam War.

While flu normally kills about 0.1 percent or one out of a thousand people, the 1918–1919 flu killed 2.5 percent of those who got it, making it twenty-five times more deadly than current flu strains. While flu killed one out of every sixty-seven members of the military, it killed fifteen times as many civilians as soldiers. A doctor in Huntsville, Alabama, reported that all pregnant women with the flu died during delivery, although a few of their babies lived.

As the pandemic finally fizzled out, scientists discovered another troubling fact. The flu, like many other infectious diseases, normally strikes the very young and the very old the hardest. Graphs showing the death toll from infectious diseases typically produce a U shape, with the high points of the U being young children and elderly people. The open part of the U represents those who are less likely to get sick—older children, teens, young adults, and adults in the prime of their lives.

The Spanish flu produced a W-shaped death chart. The first and last upper points of the W represent young children and elderly people; that's to be expected. However, the middle spike represented the death of an immense number of young adults. Worldwide, flu struck down previously healthy adults between the ages of twenty and forty with a vengeance. In fact, nearly half of the influenza-related deaths in the pandemic were in this age group. In the military, most of the dead were eighteen, nineteen, and twenty years old, more boys than men.

Among civilians, people aged twenty-five to twenty-nine were most likely to die, followed by people aged thirty to thirty-four, then those twenty to twenty-four. This generation of young people was made up of parents and workers at the peak of their productivity. The lingering trauma of death, poverty, and loss of family and livelihood affected the vitality of the world for a decade.

All but forgotten for decades, history and medical textbooks only mentioned the flu in passing. Both the press and military officials had often concealed or distorted the

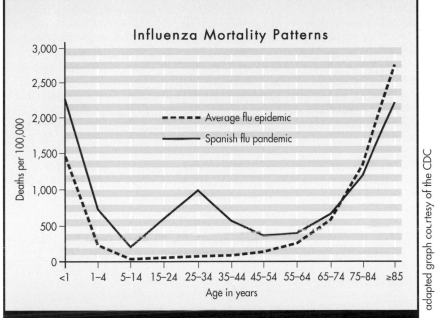

Influenza Mortality Patterns

Deaths per 100,000

- - - - Average flu epidemic
——— Spanish flu pandemic

Age in years

adapted graph courtesy of the CDC

The flu is ordinarily more lethal to the very young and the elderly, but as the point of the W in this graph indicates, the Spanish flu had a considerably higher mortality rate among teenagers and young adults.

truth. Instead of saying that a soldier died of the flu, he "died on the field of honor."

In 2003 writer and historian Alfred W. Crosby published a book about the Spanish flu titled, *America's Forgotten Pandemic*. He believed the pandemic was so wrapped up in people's minds with the horror of war that no one wanted to think about it again. The flu pandemic blended into the general nightmare of World War I. It seemed to disappear as quickly as it had come. Because the Spanish flu did not remain a constant threat like AIDS, for example, it rapidly and willingly faded from most people's memory.

MODERN PANDEMICS

While nothing has matched the virulence of the Spanish flu pandemic, lesser pandemics have hit the world twice in the second half of the twentieth century.

SECRETS FROM THE GRAVE

Even though doctors didn't know that a virus caused the terrible flu pandemic, they knew enough to save samples from its victims. Over the past 130 years, the U.S. military has collected and preserved several million samples of diseased human tissue on slides.

In 1995 American researcher Dr. Jeffrey Taubenberger began to examine the slide cultures from two soldiers who'd died of the Spanish flu. The viruses had long since disappeared. But with today's advanced laboratory techniques, Dr. Taubenberger located viral genetic material in the military samples and began working to sequence (decode) it.

Another scientist named Dr. Johan Hultin provided samples from the lungs of a woman who'd died of Spanish flu in a remote Alaskan village. Even though nearly eighty years had passed, the lung tissue had been preserved because the grave was dug in permafrost, the permanently frozen ground found in very cold climates.

Late in 2005, Dr. Taubenberger and associates announced they had completed the genetic sequencing of the 1918 flu virus from those samples. The virus was identified as H1N1, and all eight of its genes are more closely related to a bird influenza than to a human influenza. The bird virus simultaneously infected humans and pigs, rather than moving from bird to pig to human as most flu viruses do. The 1918 strain is genetically unlike any other flu virus ever examined. Tested in mice, it is one hundred times more lethal than other human flu viruses. Researchers say they still cannot be certain where the 1918 virus originated from immediately before the pandemic broke out.

- 1957–1958: Asian flu (Type A, H2N2). In 1957 the flu virus underwent antigenic shift to produce a new strain not previously seen in humans. Called the Asian flu, it was first identified in Guizhou, a province in southern China. Within a few months, it swept around the world. It's estimated that about a third of the world's population got Asian flu. Fortunately, the death rate was fairly low. However, this strain hasn't circulated in humans since 1968, so no one born since then has any immunity to it. In April 2005, a medical supply company accidentally sent out samples of this virus to laboratories around the world. WHO urged immediate destruction of the virus.

- 1968–1969: Hong Kong flu (Type A, H3N2). Another antigenic drift caused the Hong Kong flu pandemic. It was also believed to have originated in China, either in Guizhou or Yunnan Province. Because the flu first broke out in Hong Kong, the strain took its name from that city. It infected 30 million Americans and killed at least 34,000 of them. Hardest hit by the pandemic were children under five and middle-aged people between forty-five and sixty-five. Today, Type A, H3N2 is the strain most commonly circulating. Because this strain is so common, most people alive now have some degree of immunity to it.

The next flu scare began on February 4, 1976, when eighteen-year-old Private David Lewis fell ill at Fort Dix, New Jersey. At sick call that morning, a doctor sent him to bed because of fever and headache. However, Private Lewis was determined to join his unit on a 5-mile (8-km) hike that night. He started out on the hike, but he collapsed after a few miles. He died the next morning after being diagnosed with flu and pneumonia.

Shocked doctors examined throat swabs from Private Lewis and eighteen other men with the flu. Most samples showed Type A Victoria flu, the strain known to be circulating that year. The remaining samples proved to be a swine flu virus. At the time of the Fort Dix outbreak, researchers had not yet isolated the 1918 Spanish flu virus (that took nearly thirty more years), but they had identified antibodies in the blood of its survivors. At the time, it was believed the Spanish flu epidemic had started with pigs.

Spurred by memories of what had happened in 1918, health officials predicted another deadly epidemic. The U.S. government started a huge campaign to vaccinate every American against swine flu by the end of 1976. By mid-December, one-third of adult Americans had been vaccinated, along with 80 percent of the military. By late December, reports of a rare paralysis called Guillain-Barré syndrome following the swine flu shot begin to surface, and the vaccination program was halted.

In 1976 the swine flu killed one person and sickened thirteen. About five hundred people had antibodies in their blood against it, showing that they'd been exposed but had not fallen ill. All of these people lived at Fort Dix. No other cases of swine flu were ever identified. Today some historians speak of the "swine flu fiasco." Millions of dollars were spent to immunize millions of people against an epidemic that never came. The vaccine hadn't been properly tested, and over the following years, the government paid out hundreds of millions of dollars for lawsuits by people claiming to have been injured by the vaccine.

Yet government health officials were in a no-win situation. Should they have ignored what might have been an outbreak of potentially deadly flu? Or should they have done what they did—move forward with the vaccination program, even though some now accuse those officials of "crying wolf?" This becomes an important question as today's scientists predict a possible pandemic of another kind of flu in the near future.

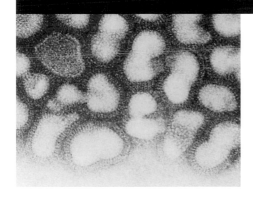

Chapter 3

THE FLU TODAY

Jake's Story

Jake has a great weekend. His team wins the basketball regional semifinals on Friday night. He takes his girlfriend, Trish, out to a party after the game. He has a good time with his dad on Saturday morning when they go to hit some golf balls at the driving range. He studies for two hours for his big history test. Jake even feels okay when he meets up with Trish at school on Monday morning.

But by lunchtime, cold chills are running through his body. His muscles ache like he's just run a marathon. His head hurts worst of all, pounding with pain. Trish takes him to the school nurse, who takes Jake's temperature. It measures a whopping 103.4°F (39.9°C). "Looks like he's got the flu that's going around," the nurse says. "We better get him

39

home." Trish calls Jake's mom on her cell phone, and thirty minutes later, he's zonked out on his living-room couch.

On Monday evening Jake's mother calls the family doctor. Jake's fever is nearly 104°F, he's coughing, and he feels so weak that he can barely sit up to drink juice. The doctor tells her that unless Jake gets worse over the next day or two, she can take care of him at home. Jake can't figure out how he got the flu. He hasn't been around any sick people.

Think you can't get the flu? Think again. WHO estimates that as many as 5 million people get bad cases of flu each year and up to half a million die of it. Millions more get milder cases. In the United States, one or two people out of every ten get the flu each year. In hard-hit communities, half the population may get sick. In the United States, about 200,000 people are hospitalized each year for flu and flu-related complications, such as pneumonia. Flu kills about 36,000 Americans each year. The number could be higher because people weakened by flu can die of related causes several weeks after they seem to recover.

While anyone can get the flu, it affects certain groups more than others:

- young children
- pregnant women
- people over sixty-five years old
- people with chronic medical conditions such as diabetes, asthma, heart and kidney disease
- people who smoke, because tobacco smoke weakens the lungs' protective defenses
- anyone with a weakened immune system, such as people with HIV/AIDS, people who have had organ transplants, and people receiving cancer treatment

People crowd a subway train in the early twenty-first century. Crowding is an ideal condition for the transmission of the influenza virus. The virus typically spreads in droplets of fluid expelled when an infected person coughs or sneezes.

FLU SEASON

Two things are sure to happen every winter: geese fly south, and the flu season comes to town. In order to thrive, flu viruses need the cooler, drier weather of winter rather than the warmer, humid weather of summer. In the United States, flu season is November through March, with the peak months being December, January, and February.

Flu strikes most often during the winter because people tend to crowd together in cold weather. They huddle inside houses and schools with the heat cranked up and the windows closed. Indoor heating dries out the mucous membranes inside our noses and throats. This makes us more susceptible to getting the flu. People riding buses and subways are sometimes jammed together so tightly there's standing room only. Crowds make it easy for the virus to spread from person to person.

41

While flu viruses do circulate all year-round, they seldom cause serious illness in the summer months. People might only get a mild fever and a runny nose. They may say they have "a little summer cold."

CATCHING IT

Here's how the flu season usually kicks off. First, school-age children get sick. Kids aged five through nine get the flu most often. Maybe it's because they have so many runny noses and they don't wash their hands very well. Kids aren't known for covering their mouths when they sneeze or cough, either! School absences rise, more people go to the doctor, and there are more hospital admissions. Then children infect their siblings and parents. The adults get sick, miss work, visit doctors, and go to the emergency room. An outbreak of flu lasts three to six weeks in a community before it moves on.

Flu has an incubation period of one to four days, meaning it takes that long before someone feels sick. During the incubation period, people can easily spread flu viruses. When people infected with a flu virus sneeze or cough, they spew out millions of viruses that float on tiny mucous droplets. Anyone inhaling those droplets has a pretty good chance of getting the flu. People can also get the flu by touching contaminated objects such as doorknobs, faucets, and chairs in the lunchroom.

Adults are generally contagious for about six days, from the day before the onset of symptoms to about five days after they get sick. Children can shed (or expel) viruses for five or six days before they have symptoms, and they can pass on flu viruses for ten or more days. People with damaged immune systems may shed flu viruses for weeks or months. But in most people, the viruses disappear from the respiratory tract within days. Even though people may still cough and sneeze, they can no longer pass the flu virus to others.

Let's follow a flu virus to see how it makes you sick. Maybe you have to go to the library to do a report about the flu. You walk through the door at 10:15 A.M. What you don't know is that a girl with the flu sneezed when she walked out the door at 10:05 A.M. So what? A sneeze can leave an invisible, infectious cloud about 25 feet (8 meters) in diameter hanging in the air for fifteen minutes or longer. You just walked through that cloud and breathed in all those viruses.

Or maybe the girl didn't sneeze. Instead, maybe a boy wiped his nose with his hand just before he opened the library door. The flu virus remains infectious anywhere from a few hours up to two days on a hard, cold surface like a metal doorknob. You touch the doorknob on your way into the library. You pick out a couple of books, sit down at a table, and pull out a notebook. Then you put your hand over your mouth, trying to hide a yawn from the librarian, because the very thought of doing a report about the flu makes you tired! Either way, by air or by touch, the flu virus has invaded your body.

Once inside your body, the flu virus makes its way to the cells lining your nose, throat, trachea, and the bronchi and bronchioles (the tiny tubes and tunnels making up your respiratory tract). Less often, the flu virus manages to get all the way down into the lungs. About fifteen minutes later, the viruses attack the epithelial cells, the layer of cells that line and protect the respiratory tract. A virus gloms onto the epithelial cell wall with its grappling hooks—the hemagglutinin spikes. It forces its way inside the cell, then turns the cell into a mean, lean, virus-producing machine.

About ten hours later, the now-dead epithelial cell bursts open to release between 1,000 and 10,000 new daughter viruses. Each daughter moves on to infect another cell. Say the first cell releases 5,000 new viruses. Those 5,000 viruses infect 5,000 new cells, releasing 25 million viruses ten hours later. The 25 million viruses each move into a new cell, producing 125 billion more in another ten hours—and that's just three generations! It takes about five or six generations of daughters (fifty to sixty hours) before you begin to realize something's wrong.

SYMPTOMS

Once the number of flu viruses reaches critical mass inside your body, you begin to feel sick. One minute you're feeling fine, and the next minute you feel like a runaway freight train hit you. The symptoms of a cold—caused by several kinds of viruses other than flu viruses—tend to come on gradually over a couple of days. The sudden onset of symptoms—often in just hours—is a specialty of the flu.

Weakness, sore throat, headache, muscle aches, runny nose, fever, chills, and a dry hacking cough are all flu symptoms. Yet it's usually not the virus itself that makes people feel sick—it's the body's own immune system responding to the viral invasion. Watery mucous in the nose helps expel viruses, as does sneezing and coughing. A sore throat occurs when white blood cells rush to the site of infection. Deep in the airways, the flu virus is destroying epithelial cells, often stripping them away entirely. As cells are destroyed, they release chemicals that travel through the bloodstream to cause bad headaches, and painful bones and muscles.

The body releases other chemicals that increase body temperature. Fever can be a good thing. It's a signal that the immune system is working at full speed to fight off infection. The fever with a bad case of flu can run from 103°F to 104°F (40°C to 40.3°C). While fever makes people feel miserable, it helps to kill viruses, which prefer cooler temperatures. Fever also increases blood flow, helping to bring body defenses to the site of infection.

Sometimes when people have nausea, vomiting, and diarrhea, they say, "I've got the stomach flu." These symptoms can be caused by dozens of different bacteria, viruses, parasites, and even toxins produced by food poisoning.

IS IT A COLD OR THE FLU?

Symptoms	Cold	Flu
Onset of symptoms	Gradual	Sudden
Fever	Rare/mild	Common, can last 3–4 days
Headache	Rare/mild	Common—may be severe
Body aches	Mild	Common—may be severe
Fatigue/weakness	Mild	Severe—may last for 2–3 weeks
Cough	Mild to moderate	Common—may be severe
Chest pain	Rare	Common
Stuffy nose	Common	Sometimes
Sneezing	Common	Sometimes
Sore throat	Common	Sometimes

About a fourth of young children who get the flu may have nausea, vomiting, and diarrhea. However, these are not usually flu symptoms in most people.

Medical historians speculate that one reason why so many young people died in the 1918–1919 flu pandemic was because of their strong immune systems. In many cases, people who suddenly died suffered from the extreme reaction of their own immune response to overwhelming infection by an entirely new virus. That seldom happens with the flu strains now circulating. Instead, the flu today is most deadly to older people. In the United States, nine out of ten people who die of flu or its complications are over sixty-five years old.

Healthy people usually recover from the flu within ten days, although they may feel weak and tired for a couple of weeks. After all, the body has a lot of repair work to do after a case of flu. It takes awhile for the immune system to build itself back up. People need to rest and take it easy until they have fully recovered. When people are in a hurry to get back to school or work, they run the risk of getting sick again.

COMPLICATIONS

A few people will develop complications during or shortly after getting over the flu. When the flu virus weakens the immune system and damages the respiratory tract, bacteria can move in. Bacterial pneumonia is the most common complication of the flu. Most flu-related deaths are due to bacterial pneumonia. Even with today's powerful antibiotics, bacterial pneumonia can be deadly. Many kinds of bacteria are becoming resistant to antibiotics that used to kill them. Other less common flu complications include ear infections, meningitis (swelling of the membranes around the brain and spinal cord), and encephalitis (swelling of the brain itself).

One or two people out of one hundred thousand develop a rare neurological disorder called Guillain-Barré syndrome two to three weeks after recovering from the flu. Guillain-Barré paralyzes muscles starting from the legs and going up. If the paralysis reaches the diaphragm, people must be put on machines called ventilators to breath for them. Doctors believe the disorder is an overactive immune response to the viral infection. Most people with

Guillain-Barré recover; it has a mortality rate of less than 5 percent. About 10 to 20 percent of people are left with some permanent paralysis. The rest gradually recover from the paralysis over several months.

In 1976 doctors reported an increase in the numbers of people developing Guillain-Barré syndrome after getting vaccinated for swine flu. While it was never conclusively proven that the swine flu vaccine caused the disorder, health officials were worried enough to stop the vaccination program.

These are some common warning signs of flu complications that require immediate medical attention:

In children:
- won't drink enough fluids (might lead to dehydration)
- fast breathing or labored breathing (could be a sign of pneumonia)
- bluish color around the lips, fingertips, or nails (could be a sign of not getting enough oxygen because of pneumonia)
- seizures (sometimes occur due to high fever or encephalitis)
- not waking up or not acting normally (could be a sign of meningitis, encephalitis, or severe dehydration)
- extreme irritability, child doesn't want to be held or consoled (same as above)
- fever with a rash (could be a sign of another infectious disease, such as measles or meningococcal meningitis, because flu doesn't cause a rash)
- flu symptoms improve but then return with fever and worsening cough (could be a sign of bacterial pneumonia)

In adults:
- difficulty breathing or shortness of breath (could be a sign of pneumonia)

- sputum gets thick and turns green or yellow green (could be a sign of bacterial pneumonia)
- pain or pressure in the chest or abdomen (could be a sign of pneumonia or heart problems)
- sudden dizziness (might mean dehydration or neurological problem)
- confusion (same as above)

Even though the flu still remains a dangerous foe today, we have medications to help prevent it and to treat its symptoms. The next chapter will discuss the two types of flu vaccines and common sense measures to keep from getting the flu.

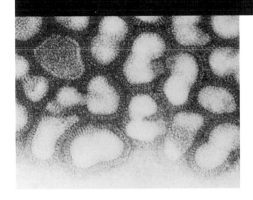

Chapter 4

PREVENT THE FLU

Daveon's Story

Daveon is really tired of having asthma. He puffs from an inhaler in the morning before school and when he gets home in the afternoon. He takes a pill every night along with his breathing treatment. He carries a special emergency inhaler in his backpack in case he has an asthma attack at school. Other kids at school sometimes see him using his medication and ask about it. The school nurse keeps a medical record about him. "Seems like everybody knows my business," he grumbles.

But the worst part of having asthma according to Daveon is that he has to get a flu shot every fall. "No other kid my age has to get the shot," he complains. "My doctor says I have pretty bad asthma, and that if I got the flu I could get plenty sick. But I'm real young. Only old people need flu shots, right? Can't talk Mom out of it, though. Every year right after Halloween she marches me down to the doctor's office to get my shot."

People have been trying to prevent disease for a very long time. About 2,600 years ago, Chinese doctors blew powdered smallpox scabs into people's noses in an attempt to prevent the disease. In the Middle East, a quill dipped in powdered scabs was scratched across skin, a practice called inoculation. While some people surely got smallpox, using the scabs in this manner prevented it much of the time. Even though people didn't understand how smallpox inoculations worked, Europeans tried it out as early as 1718. Americans started a few years later. During the Revolutionary War (1775–1783), George Washington had all his troops successfully inoculated against smallpox.

English physician Edward Jenner was the first person to understand and demonstrate the science behind smallpox inoculation. He'd noticed that milkmaids who caught cowpox, a disease similar to smallpox but much milder, never seemed to get smallpox. He believed that getting cowpox somehow made the milkmaids immune to smallpox. In 1796 he broke a cowpox blister on a milkmaid's wrist, then scratched the fluid into the skin of a healthy eight-year-old boy named James Phipps.

James developed cowpox, just as Dr. Jenner wanted him to. A few weeks later after he'd recovered, Dr. Jenner inoculated James with pus from a smallpox victim. The boy did not get smallpox. Such a dangerous experiment would never be allowed today, but it did prove that being vaccinated with cowpox prevented smallpox. It was a lot safer than using scabs from actual smallpox victims. Dr. Jenner called his procedure *vaccinia* from *vacca*, the Latin word for *cow*. We call it vaccination.

Today, vaccinations prevent illness and death in millions of people every year. Children are routinely vaccinated against diseases such as polio, chicken pox, mumps,

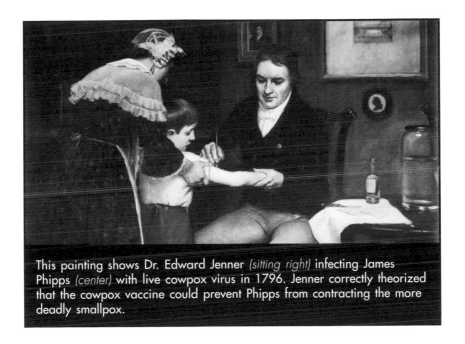

This painting shows Dr. Edward Jenner *(sitting right)* infecting James Phipps *(center)* with live cowpox virus in 1796. Jenner correctly theorized that the cowpox vaccine could prevent Phipps from contracting the more deadly smallpox.

diphtheria, measles, tetanus, and whooping cough by the time they are two years old. Travelers can be vaccinated against diseases such as yellow fever and cholera before visiting countries where those diseases are common. More than fifty vaccines are licensed for use in the United States to prevent infectious diseases, including the flu.

PROVING THE CAUSE

Scientists started working on a vaccine to prevent flu during the Spanish flu pandemic. Even though doctors didn't yet know flu was caused by a virus, they were skilled at developing vaccines for other diseases. They hoped to do the same with flu. Researchers were pretty sure that whatever caused the flu was spread in the air and in the mucous of people who had it. But before they could make a vaccine, they had to prove how flu was passed.

In November 1918, a group of U.S. military prisoners volunteered to become guinea pigs in return for freedom by letting doctors give them the flu on purpose. Doctors collected mucous from soldiers sick with the flu. They sprayed secretions into the eyes, nose, and throats of the healthy volunteers. Doctors drew blood from flu victims and injected it into the same volunteers. The healthy men were told to lean over sick men and breathe in the foul air they exhaled. Sick men coughed into their faces. Nothing worked. The volunteers didn't get sick. Even though doctors tried everything they could think of, not a single healthy man got the flu.

Experiments were repeated at other military facilities. None of the healthy men got flu from the sick men! Today, researchers believe the healthy men were immune to the flu because they'd developed antibodies after recovering from a mild case of it. Or it could be that the experiments were performed after the flu virus had already left the bodies of its victims so that they were no longer infectious.

Doctors turned to experiments on animals—monkeys, baboons, rabbits, and guinea pigs (real ones this time). In 1930 American bacteriologist Richard E. Shope succeeded in transmitting flu between pigs. Doctors applauded his work. But we must thank ferrets for the first real breakthrough in human flu research. In 1933 three British scientists transmitted flu from a sick human to ferrets. The sick ferrets transmitted it to healthy ferrets. When a sick ferret sneezed on one of the scientists, he got the flu. The infectious circle was complete.

The British researchers then showed that flu could be prevented by dripping diluted secretions from human or ferret flu victims into the noses of healthy ferrets. The first primitive flu vaccine had been developed! By 1941 scientists had proved that a vaccine could prevent flu or at least lessen its severity. The first flu vaccine was developed to protect soldiers during World War II. These early vaccines often contained impurities that produced fever, headaches, and other side effects, leading to the mistaken belief that the vaccine could cause flu.

THE FLU SHOT

The flu vaccination has been safely used for over sixty years. Today, over 90 million Americans get flu shots each fall. How successful the flu vaccination is at preventing the flu depends on three factors:

- the age of the recipient: Older children, teens, and adults have a better response and are less likely to get the flu after being vaccinated for it than are very young children and adults over sixty-five years old.

- the strength of the immune system: People of any age with strong immune systems form more antibodies against flu, making them less likely to get it.

- how closely the vaccine matches circulating strains of flu: The flu viruses circulating in the spring when the vaccine formula is developed are likely to mutate to some extent by the time people get vaccinated in the fall, so that the vaccine is seldom an exact match.

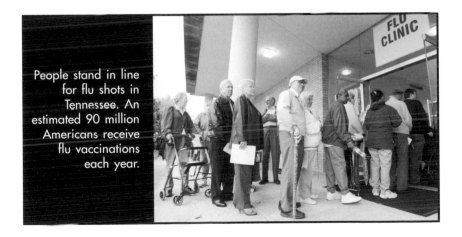

People stand in line for flu shots in Tennessee. An estimated 90 million Americans receive flu vaccinations each year.

In healthy teens and adults, the flu shot prevents flu 70 to 90 percent of the time. However, the flu vaccination is less effective among children under nine years old. For maximum protection, these children must receive two shots spaced one month apart the first year they get vaccinated. In people over sixty-five years old, the flu shot reduces illness by about 60 percent and flu-related deaths by 70 to 80 percent. Even when immunized people get the flu, their symptoms are likely to be much milder than people who didn't get the immunization.

Each February experts at WHO meet to decide on the recipe for the flu vaccine for the Northern Hemisphere. Another recommendation is made in September for the vaccine for the Southern Hemisphere. The scientists make their best guess as to what strains of viruses will be circulating by winter.

The vaccine includes killed viruses or fragments of killed viruses for two Type A strains and one Type B strain. For example, the Northern Hemisphere vaccine for the 2005–2006 flu season contained A/New Caledonia/

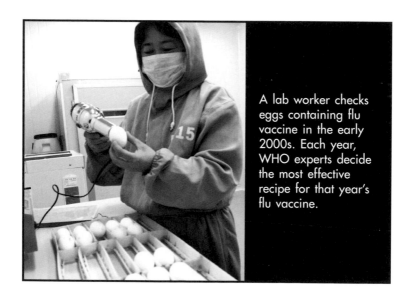

A lab worker checks eggs containing flu vaccine in the early 2000s. Each year, WHO experts decide the most effective recipe for that year's flu vaccine.

H1N1, A/California/H3N2, and B/Shanghai. Sometimes a strain of flu will turn up in the winter that was not predicted to surface. By then it's too late to make any changes to the year's vaccine. Even so, the vaccine will offer some protection against the other strains because the viruses have some similarities.

WHEN, WHERE, AND WHO?

It takes the human immune system about two weeks after vaccination to develop antibodies against the flu. The Centers for Disease Control and Prevention (CDC) recommends getting vaccinated between October 1 and November 15 of each year. However, later vaccination may still be helpful. During the flu vaccine shortages of 2004–2005 and 2005–2006, the CDC recommended vaccination through February.

The flu shot is given deep into a muscle. Children under two years old are injected in the upper thigh. For the rest of us, the flu shot is given into the deltoid muscle of the upper arm. The needle must be at least an inch long to deliver the medication deep into the muscle. People with excess fat over their muscles may need longer needles. While no one likes to get shots, the discomfort only lasts for a few seconds.

Local reactions such as redness, swelling, warmth, and pain at the injection site affect between one-tenth and two-thirds of patients. The reaction is mild and generally lasts one or two days. The painful swelling can be easily treated with intermittent cold compresses placed over the injection site.

Some people have a systemic reaction—a bodywide reaction that includes fever, fatigue, and muscle aches after a flu shot. About one out of ten children under five have such reactions, especially with their first flu shot. Among healthy young people between eleven and fifteen, only 5 percent have any kind of systemic reaction.

It's important to understand that the flu shot cannot give anyone the flu. It's impossible because the vaccine is made of dead viruses. Yet one-third of the people who took a survey in 2004 said they believed that the flu shot can cause the flu. When people have flulike symptoms after getting a flu shot, they may be having a normal reaction, they may actually have a cold, or they might have caught the flu in spite of the shot. Even though the shots are not 100 percent effective at preventing flu, they save lives and decrease the severity of illness, especially in high-risk people.

The CDC periodically updates its list of who should receive the injectable flu vaccination. (There's another kind of flu vaccination described below). For example, during the 2005–2006 flu season, the recommendations about who should get vaccinated were:

People at increased risk for flu complications:
- people aged sixty-five years and older
- residents of nursing homes and other facilities where people with chronic medical conditions live
- adults and children who have chronic heart or lung problems (including asthma and emphysema)
- adults and children who have other chronic conditions, such as diabetes, kidney disease, sickle-cell disease, or an impaired immune system (includes HIV)
- children and adolescents aged six months to eighteen years who take daily aspirin for certain medical conditions
- women who will be pregnant during flu season
- healthy children aged six months to twenty-three months (younger babies will be protected by their mothers' immune systems if they are breast-fed)

Others:
- adults aged fifty to sixty-four years old
- doctors, nurses, paramedics, and other health-care workers

- people who take care of high-risk people at home or in nursing homes
- family members living with or caring for an infant under six months old
- people in the general population who want to decrease their risk of getting the flu; this includes healthy children, teens, and adults under fifty.

THE NASAL SPRAY

For people who hate shots, there's a newer form of flu immunization—a nasal spray. In 2003 the Food and Drug Administration (FDA) approved the medication called Flu-Mist for healthy people between five and forty-nine years old. This vaccine is made from live viruses treated to weaken them so they cannot cause flu in healthy people. Because people who receive the spray may shed viruses for a few days, it's not recommended for anyone in contact with people who have weak immune systems. It's also not approved for use in people of any age who have asthma or other chronic diseases such as diabetes or kidney problems, or for pregnant women.

The flu spray is easy and convenient to use. It comes in a prefilled spray device that looks somewhat like a thin syringe but without a needle. A health-care worker sprays 0.25 millimeter (just a few drops) of the vaccine into each nostril. Side effects are mild. Children can get a runny or stuffy nose, headache, or fever. Adults have similar reactions but get a sore throat more often than fever.

There are some oral prescription medications that have proved useful in helping to prevent influenza. These antiviral medications are *not* a replacement for the vaccine, which is much more effective. The antivirals only *help* to prevent flu. Because the medications are more widely used to treat flu or are given to someone who has been exposed, they will be reviewed in the next chapter on treatment.

SCRAMBLED EGGS

The world's supply of flu vaccine starts out with two legs and a bunch of feathers. The source of the vaccine is not a chemical manufacturer but a chicken farmer. Unlike bacteria, flu viruses won't readily grow in a culture dish or a test tube. Flu viruses don't need food; they require living cells to reproduce. The viruses needed to prepare the flu vaccine (both the injectable and nasal spray) are grown inside fertilized chicken eggs. The process starts in August of the year *before* the flu vaccine reaches your doctor's office.

- August — Special white leghorn hens lay their eggs. They hatch in twenty-one days.
- September — The chicks are moved into large buildings where they can roam freely. They take three months to grow up.
- December — The now-mature hens mate with roosters and start laying fertile eggs, about one per day. Hens can lay eggs for about nine months until they get too old.
- January — The fertile eggs (which would hatch into chickens if hens sat on them) are collected by the chicken farmer and incubated for seven to twelve days. Then the eggs are delivered to the vaccine manufacturer.
- February — The WHO releases the names of the three flu strains it believes will be circulating in the fall.

- February–   The vaccine makers go to work. A
  September   machine punches a hole in each egg and
  a needle injects a single virus strain. The
  virus multiples for three days. The egg
  is broken, and the fluid around the
  chicken embryo is collected and purified. The strains must be grown in sepa-
  rate eggs before being combined to
  make the final vaccine. It takes about
  270 million eggs to make the 90 million
  doses of vaccine used in the United
  States each year (one egg per virus
  strain, three strains per dose).
- May–   The vaccine maker sends vaccine
  June   samples to the FDA for tests, while con-
  tinuing to perform its own testing.
- September   The vaccine manufacturer finishes making the final doses.
- October   The vaccine is distributed in October.
  Millions of Americans head to flu clin-
  ics and doctors' offices to get vaccinated
  against the flu.

The flu vaccine can be dangerous for people who
are allergic to eggs. Those people should never receive
the injectable or nasal spray vaccine without their doctors' approval. During a flu epidemic, people with egg
allergies should ask their doctors if they can take
antiviral medications to help prevent the flu.

THE BASICS

Old-fashioned common sense can go a long way toward preventing flu. Here are three easy rules to remember during flu season.

- Stay home: Too often people who feel sick continue to go to school or work. Maybe there's a big test coming up or a party. Maybe you're worried about missing a day from your weekend job. It's bad for everyone when sick people spread the flu around. Staying home keeps you from infecting other people. It also lets you get the rest your body needs while it works to fight off the flu. Staying home a few days after the flu can help you recover from the fatigue that so often follows. Don't visit people who are home sick with flu. Phone or e-mail them instead.

- Cover up: Cover your mouth and nose when coughing or sneezing, and ask others to do the same. Use a tissue once, then throw it away. If you don't have a tissue, hold your arm across your face when you cough or sneeze. That's better than using your hand. If you cough into your hand, you spread viruses to everything you touch.

- Wash your hands: One of the best things you can do to keep from getting the flu is to thoroughly wash your hands. Soap interacts with water to loosen dirt, bacteria, and viruses from your skin. Use plenty of soap and warm running water. Wash for twenty seconds. That's about as long as it takes to sing the "Happy Birthday" song twice. Scrub your palms, the backs of your hands, wrists, and between your fingers. Remember to wash under your fingernails. In public restrooms, use a paper towel to turn off the faucet and to open the door when you leave. Alcohol-based hand sanitizers do a good job when you have to clean your hands without water. Tuck a few packets of hand wipes into your backpack so you'll be ready to wash up anywhere. People who are responsible for young children must remind them to wash their hands or help them to do it. Wash your own hands after using the bathroom, before eating, before preparing food, after caring for young children, and after touching surfaces in public places (such as doorknobs, faucets, and shopping carts). Avoid touching your eyes, nose, and mouth with unwashed hands during flu season.

Flu causes millions of days lost from school and work each year. Even when people do all the right things, such as getting the flu vaccine, washing their hands, and staying away from sick people, they may get the flu anyway. Fortunately, treatments are now available that were unknown just a few years ago. Read on to learn about some of them.

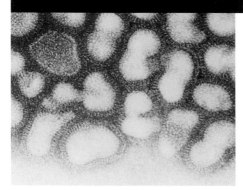

Chapter 5

TREAT THE FLU

Ben's Story

Sometimes Ben feels like it's his job to take care of his grandma Rose. His dad lives in another state, and it seems like his mom works all the time. Grandma Rose doesn't always take her diabetes medications on time, and she sneaks outside to smoke every chance she gets. Every morning Ben hears her hacking and coughing from her room, and it really worries him.

Ben sees a story on TV that says people with diabetes should get their flu shots. When he talks to his grandmother about it, she says, "Ben, I got a flu shot once, and it gave me the flu. I'm never getting another one! Besides, I'm pretty healthy." Ben knows she isn't healthy at all, but nothing he says makes any difference to his stubborn grandmother.

Ben doesn't get the flu this year, but he carries it home to Grandma Rose. When Rose first gets sick, her doctor gives her the antiviral medication Tamiflu, but it doesn't help much. A few days later, Ben's mother takes Rose to the hospital where she's admitted and treated for bacterial pneumonia. She stays in the hospital for ten days, and it takes her three months to fully recover.

Sometimes even when people get their flu shots, stay away from sick friends, and take care of themselves, they still come down with the flu. Many people never seek medical help when they get the flu, nor do they need to. They climb into bed, drink lots of fluids, and take something for the fever and aches. For most people, that's enough.

People who don't get better in a few days or those whose symptoms are severe (described in chapter 3) should see their doctor or go to a hospital emergency room. Anyone who has a chronic medical condition (for example, people with diabetes, heart or lung disease, kidney disease, cancer, or HIV) should consult a doctor as well. Older adults and parents of sick infants should check in with their doctors to ask if they need to be seen. Once people seek medical care, the doctor must determine if the patient has the flu or not before recommending any treatment. That's trickier than it seems.

MAKING THE DIAGNOSIS

Many kinds of viruses and some bacteria cause symptoms similar to flu, such as weakness, cough, fever, runny nose, sore throat, and aches. A doctor may decide a patient probably has the flu based on the pattern of symptoms, how quickly they came on, whether or not it's flu season, and whether or not flu has been reported in the area. During flu season, the Centers for Disease Control and Prevention issues a weekly report detailing the location and

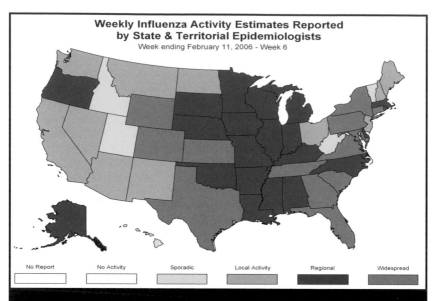

Weekly Influenza Activity Estimates Reported by State & Territorial Epidemiologists
Week ending February 11, 2006 - Week 6

No Report | No Activity | Sporadic | Local Activity | Regional | Widespread

The CDC maintains a weekly flu activity report that helps doctors and scientists monitor the spread of the illness. Part of the report, this map shows influenza activity in the United States for the week ending February 11, 2006.

number of suspected and confirmed cases. If hundreds of people in a community have already been diagnosed with the flu, a doctor is more likely to suspect the flu in a new patient than if no cases have been identified.

Doctors do not need to perform tests on all patients in order to diagnose the flu and give advice about how to treat it. Tests are most useful when the doctor is uncertain if someone has the flu or another illness. If a test confirms the flu, antiviral medications may be prescribed (discussed in next section). If a patient has flulike symptoms but the flu test is negative, the doctor may decide to treat the patient with antibiotics for a possible bacterial infection.

Sometimes doctors test patients for the flu as part of a broader community-based surveillance. In other words, the results may not be as important for the individual patient as they are for the community. Testing may be done:

- within a hospital or nursing home when flu is suspected to help prevent an outbreak among patients

- to establish which strain of flu is circulating in a community at a given time—this can tell doctors if the vaccine formula is well matched to circulating viruses

- to help predict what strains might be circulating in the future in order to develop the vaccine for next season

Most flu tests require a mucous sample. A health-care worker takes a swab similar to a long-handled Q-tip and scrapes it along the back of the throat. It's a lot like getting a throat swab to see if you have strep throat. Sometimes the inside of the nose is swabbed as well or flushed with a salt-water solution. The samples must be collected during the first four days of illness in order to be certain that live viruses are still present.

A doctor or laboratory has choices when it comes to flu tests. There are several kinds of rapid diagnostic tests. They are strip tests, similar to home pregnancy tests, except the strip is dipped in mucous instead of urine. Some tests only identify whether the flu is Type A or B, while others can detect either kind. Although results are available in about thirty minutes, some of the tests produce a high rate of false negatives, meaning that the person actually has flu even though the test is negative.

Doctors also can test for flu viruses by measuring viral RNA and antibodies. It only takes four to six hours to accurately identify the viral RNA—the genetic material in the sample. Antibodies to flu can be measured in the blood. An increase in antibodies to a strain of flu between a sample taken when the person is sick and a sample taken two weeks later proves that the person had that strain.

Another way to identify a specific flu virus is by viral culture. Viruses can only be cultured, or grown, inside living cells. At the laboratory, technicians use the human mucous samples to infect fertile eggs, or kidney cells from dogs or monkeys. That doesn't mean an animal has to be killed for each test—animal kidney cells can be grown in the laboratory for years. It takes three to ten days for the virus to grow. Then the cells can be tested for viral proteins or viral RNA. Some infectious disease doctors discourage the culturing of flu viruses because of the possibility of a laboratory accident. If that happened, flu viruses could be released into the environment. That could be dangerous if the viruses were a new strain.

While several of these tests take too long to benefit a particular patient, they allow public health officials to track the spread of flu through a community. This is the only way to determine the exact strain, such as A/H3N2—the strain most commonly circulating at present. Keeping track of flu strains allows doctors to develop the vaccine for the next season and to plan for future outbreaks or epidemics.

TREATING THE FLU

Even if people don't need to see a doctor, they should take good care of themselves. Anyone recovering from the flu needs a lot of rest, preferably at home in bed. The person needs to drink plenty of fluids, such as water and juice to combat the dehydrating effects of illness and fever. Over-the-counter (OTC) flu and cold medications can temporarily help coughs and stuffy or runny noses. Acetaminophen (the ingredient in Tylenol), ibuprofen (the ingredient in Advil and Motrin), and aspirin can reduce fever and relieve aches and pains. *However, no one under nineteen years old should take aspirin for flu symptoms without a doctor's specific approval.*

Anyone who takes prescription medications or who has a medical condition should consult with a pharmacist or a doctor before taking OTC medications. They are not safe for everyone and may cause serious side effects in some people. Some cold medications, for example, may temporarily increase blood pressure, making them unsafe for people with high blood pressure. Be sure to follow the instructions on the package when taking any OTC medication.

Flu can't be cured in the usual sense, unlike strep throat, for example. A doctor gives an antibiotic such as penicillin to a child with strep throat. The medication cures the child by killing the *Streptococcus pyogenes* bacteria that cause strep throat. However, antibiotics won't cure the flu because they only work against bacteria.

One group of prescription drugs called antiviral medications has proven useful in treating the flu. Doctors may prescribe them for people with bad cases of flu or for those with chronic medical conditions who are at high risk for flu complications. Some of the medications are not widely available or are expensive. Because flu viruses are beginning to show resistance to the medications, doctors may be reluctant to prescribe them for normally healthy people with the flu.

While antiviral medications will not cure the flu, they may shorten the length of illness by a day or two and lesson the severity of symptoms. To be effective, the medications must be started before the onset of symptoms or within forty-eight hours after they start. Like other prescription medications, antivirals may have unwanted side effects and some people may be allergic to them.

Unlike antibiotics such as penicillin, which are used to treat several kinds of bacterial infections, antiviral medications are very specific for particular viruses. Antiviral medications are available to treat such viral infections as HIV, herpes, hepatitis, and influenza. Only four antiviral medications are currently approved for the *treatment* of flu. There are two kinds that work in different ways.

The first type of antiviral medications are entry blockers. They prevent viruses from releasing their RNA into host cells. This stops the viruses from replicating.

These medications are only effective against Type A flu and include:

- Flumadine (generic name, rimantadine) is only approved for adults. It comes in tablets and syrup. It's used for at least seven days. Flumadine may cause headaches, dizziness, fatigue, nervousness, low blood pressure, ringing in the ears, nausea, vomiting, diarrhea, loss of appetite, and rash.

- Symmetrel (generic name, amantadine) is approved for people one year old and up. It comes in tablets, liquid-filled capsules, and syrup. It's given daily until one to two days after symptoms have gone. Symmetrel has also been used for years to treat the symptoms of Parkinson's disease. It has a long list of potentially serious side effects and is used less often than the other antiviral medications.

The second type of antiviral medications are neuraminidase inhibitors. They prevent new viruses from being released and moving on to infect other cells. The medications bind to the viral neuraminidase so that when new viruses break out of the dead host cell, the daughter viruses clump up or get trapped on the cell's surface. They're effective against both Type A and Type B flu strains and include:

- Tamiflu (generic name, oseltamivir) is approved for people one year old and up. It comes in capsules and a powder to be mixed with water. It's taken for five days. Tamiflu may cause headaches, dizziness, fatigue, nausea, vomiting, and diarrhea.

- Relenza (generic name, zanamivir) is approved for people seven years old and up. It comes in a powder, which is inhaled using a special inhaler device. It's taken for five days. Relenza may cause headaches, dizziness, ringing in the ears, nausea, vomiting, and diarrhea.

Tamiflu, Flumadine, and Symmetrel have also proved useful in helping to *prevent* the flu. When used for preventive purposes, all three medications are approved for use in anyone who is one year of age or older. Antiviral medications are *not* a replacement for the flu vaccine. While antivirals can prevent flu and lessen its severity, they are not as effective as the vaccine.

Antiviral medications may be used for prevention during flu outbreaks for the few weeks it takes the immune system to develop antibodies in response to the vaccine. If supplies are available, they also can be taken during flu outbreaks by both vaccinated and unvaccinated people when extra protection is needed. They may be used during shortages of flu vaccine, as occurred during the 2004–2005 flu season and, to a lesser extent, during 2005–2006. Because people allergic to eggs should not receive flu vaccinations, antiviral medications offer an alternative means of protection.

In January 2006, the CDC announced that doctors should no longer prescribe Flumadine or Symmetrel to prevent or treat flu. H3N2, the most common strain of flu circulating today, has become highly resistant to the medications. In 2004–2005, only 11 percent of H3N2 specimens tested were resistant to Flumadine and Symmetrel. Specimens tested during the 2005–2006 season showed that 91 percent were resistant to the medications. Two weeks later, a major medical journal recommended that Tamiflu and Relenza not be used for H3N2. The researchers said the medications should be reserved for use in a possible flu pandemic.

TREATING COMPLICATIONS

Sometimes people recover from the flu only to come down with another illness in a week or so. Flu temporarily weakens the immune system, allowing bacterial infections to set in. People need to see their doctors if they develop new symptoms after getting over the flu. Signs of a possible

REYE'S SYNDROME

Reye's syndrome is a rare and potentially fatal disorder linked to taking aspirin during viral illnesses such as influenza and chicken pox. Symptoms usually develop about a week after the viral illness and include persistent vomiting, fever, and confusion. Liver and brain damage may occur within a few days.

Reye's syndrome usually affects children between four and sixteen years old. About 20 to 30 percent of people who develop Reye's die, and others may be left with permanent brain damage. During the 1960s, 1970s, and early 1980s, the CDC estimated between 600 and 1,200 cases of Reye's syndrome occurred each year.

Around 1980 scientists discovered the connection between viral illness, aspirin, and Reye's syndrome. In 1982 the United States surgeon general, the Food and Drug Administration, and the American Academy of Pediatrics jointly issued warnings about giving aspirin to children. The number of people developing Reye's syndrome has plummeted to just a few cases a year.

To be on the safe side, many doctors today advise against giving aspirin to children and young people under nineteen for *any* reason. Dozens of OTC products and numerous cold and sinus remedies contain aspirin. Read labels carefully. The list of ingredients may include acetylsalicylate or salicylic; both are terms for aspirin. Children and adolescents should not take aspirin-containing medications without the specific permission of their doctor.

bacterial infection could include a fever that returns after it's been gone for a few days or mucous from the lungs or nose that turns from clear or white to yellow or green. A new sore throat or bad earache also may signal the onset of a bacterial infection.

A doctor will likely prescribe antibiotics when a probable bacterial infection has developed in someone who has recovered from the flu. Doctors must be very careful to prescribe antibiotics only for bacterial infections. Antibiotics won't help the flu, and taking them unnecessarily contributes to the development of antibiotic-resistant bacteria. About six out of ten people stop taking antibiotics when they start feeling better. When that happens, the strongest bacteria are still alive. They continue to reproduce, and their offspring will be more resistant to the antibiotic in the future. That's bad for all of us.

Antibiotics are so important that they have their own set of rules. If your doctor prescribes antibiotics because you got a bacterial infection after the flu, be sure to take them exactly as prescribed and for as long as prescribed. Don't share them with other people, even if it seems like they have the same illness as you. Don't demand antibiotics from your doctor or ask for a specific one because you heard it is better. Trust your doctor to prescribe the right antibiotic for the bacteria that's making you sick.

As we'll read in the next chapter, many scientists are warning the world that a new type of flu called bird flu may well cause the next pandemic. Yet, just at a time when we might need every weapon in our medical arsenal, doctors have discovered that flu viruses are developing resistance to antiviral medications in the same way that bacteria are becoming resistant to antibiotics. Read on to learn why the innocent-sounding bird flu is so very dangerous.

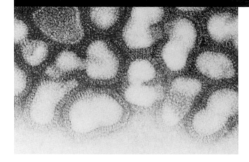

Chapter 6

BIRD FLU: SKIPPING THE PIG

Linh's Story

Linh knows she is luckier than many girls her age in Vietnam. The ducks and chickens her family raise provide eggs and meat. And when the birds and extra eggs are sold at market, Linh's mother can buy plenty of rice and vegetables. There's even enough money so that Linh and her little brother, Loc, can get the clothing and books they need for school.

One morning Linh notices some of the chickens look sick. They're coughing and having trouble breathing. In just a few hours, forty of them are dead. The next day, village health officials come to tell Linh's father that all two hundred of the chickens must be killed. Linh's mother cries as the workers collect and kill every chicken. "What will I feed my children? How will we buy rice?" Men in rubber masks spray the house and yard with disinfectant.

Two days later, Loc gets very sick. He has a fever, a cough, and trouble breathing, like the chickens did. Just before the chickens got sick, Linh and Loc helped their parents prepare two dozen chickens for the market in Ho Chi Minh City. Linh wonders if the chickens made her brother sick. Her mother takes the little boy to the regional hospital.

Linh and her father are stunned when the health officials return to their farm a few days later to say that all their ducks must be killed as well. No one will be allowed to raise ducks in Vietnam until the bird disease can be controlled. How will they live? The government gives them a little money, but it won't last long. Even worse news arrives when Linh's mother comes home that afternoon to tell the family that Loc died in the hospital. Linh didn't even have a chance to say good-bye.

H5N1. Remember it. H5N1 is not the name of a hot new rapper, a grunge band, or the model number of the latest running shoe. It's the name of a strain of flu that until a few years ago was only found in birds. In 1997 this particular strain of shape-shifting flu virus crossed over from chickens to infect a human being for the very first time. Scientists call H5N1 avian or bird flu.

Since 1997 bird flu has killed fewer than 150 people, all of them in Asian, Middle Eastern, or Eastern European countries. That doesn't seem like such a big deal. After all, it is thousands of miles away. The big deal is that bird flu kills nearly half of everyone it infects. That makes it one of the worst diseases known to man.

When epidemiologists study the history of influenza over the past two hundred years, they notice that a pandemic occurs about every thirty years on average. It happens when a strain of flu virus undergoes an antigenic shift, a sudden and radical genetic mutation. The last flu pandemic occurred more than thirty-five years ago, during the winter of 1968–1969. World health officials say that we are overdue for a flu pandemic. They predict it will certainly come within the next few years, and they predict it will be caused by bird flu.

NO PIGS NEED APPLY

It's time for a quick review of chapter 1. Do you remember the flu virus? It looks somewhat like a dandelion spiked with about six hundred hemagglutinin and neuraminidase antigens. There are sixteen known subtypes of H antigens and nine subtypes of N. Type A flu viruses are named for their H and N subtypes. The danger of a particular flu strain depends on which subtype of H and N make it up, and whether or not a population has any natural immunity to it.

Remember also that scientists think all strains of flu are carried by wild migrating waterfowl, especially ducks and geese. Often the birds settle down for a stopover in Asia where people live in close proximity to their birds and pigs. Maybe they appreciate the numerous ponds and waterways or maybe they just want to scrounge up a meal of chicken feed. Whatever the reason, the wild birds pass the virus on to domesticated chickens. Who pass it to pigs. Who pass it to people. Who pass it on to other people.

Until a few years ago, scientists believed flu could not move directly from birds to people without passing through pigs. Pigs and people have very similar respiratory tracts. As far as flu viruses go, pigs bridge the gap between birds and humans. Pity the pigs. They can get flu from birds, from one another, and even from people!

Once inside pigs, bird flu viruses mix and mingle (or re-assort) their genes with other flu viruses, turning them into viruses that can easily infect humans. Genetic studies of the viruses that caused the three flu pandemics of the twentieth century (1918, 1957, and 1968) suggest that all the viruses moved from birds through pigs before being able to infect people. There was no reason to suspect that flu viruses could move directly from birds to people. An intermediary host seemed necessary.

However, in 2005, after scientists had successfully sequenced the 1918 virus, they discovered that virus was indeed a bird flu virus. It had moved from birds to infect people and pigs at the same time. It appears that flu viruses don't always require a pig as a place for genetic reassortment. It seems that humans themselves can serve as an alternative mixing bowl. Scientists are especially worried about the new guy in town, the virus named H5N1, a dangerous virus that somehow skips the pig and goes straight to people.

THE FIRST CASES

Case #1: In May 1997, a three-year-old boy in Hong Kong fell sick with the flu. At first, it seemed like it was "just the flu," so his parents kept him home from preschool and gave him aspirin for the fever and aches. In a few days, he developed pneumonia and was admitted to the hospital. The toddler got worse and doctors hooked him up to a ventilator. His liver stopped working and his brain swelled up—symptoms of Reye's syndrome caused by the aspirin he received.

The child died on May 21, 1997, of Reye's. However, doctors worried about the flu that had started it all. Why had a healthy little boy gotten so sick? Health officials sent blood and tissue samples to specialized laboratories around the world, including the CDC in Atlanta. By mid-August, researchers had the answer—a strain of bird flu known as H5N1 was what originally made the child sick. Teachers recalled that the boy had played with chicks and ducklings in the "feathered pet corner" of his preschool. Every bird died right around the time the child got sick.

Doctors were stunned! No human being had ever been known to be infected with H5N1.

Case #2: On November 6, 1997, another little boy in Hong Kong got sick; this one was two years old. He started out with a sore throat, a fever, and cough. The next day, he was so sick he had to be admitted to the hospital. He recovered and went home two days later. A nasal swab showed the child also had H5N1 bird flu. The doctors never figured out how he got sick or why he was lucky enough to recover.

Over the next few weeks, sixteen more people got bird flu and a third of them died, all from a strain of flu never before seen in people. One case especially alarmed health-care workers. A five-year-old girl whose grand-mother scavenged dead chickens for the family dinner table got sick. It seemed obvious that she got bird flu from the diseased birds. But two cousins of the little girl also got bird flu, apparently not from sick chickens, but probably from contact with their sick cousin. This was the first time that doctors suspected bird flu might be passed from person to person.

Scientists tested a sample of chickens sold in public markets. One out of ten tested positive for H5N1 bird flu. On December 28, 1997, the Chinese government made a very difficult decision. It ordered every bird sold for food in Hong Kong markets—1.5 million birds—to be destroyed in order to stop the spread of bird flu.

Farmers and market vendors scuffled with health offi-cials and reporters. Government workers put on white coveralls and donned face masks as they prepared for the slaughter. Chickens, ducks, geese, pigeons, turkeys, and quail were grabbed by the feet, jammed into black plastic bags, then gassed with carbon dioxide. When the gas ran out, knives were used.

It must have been like a scene from a nightmare—thousands and thousands of birds squawking in terror, fly-ing feathers, screaming people, the hiss of gas, sprays of blood shooting through the air. It took less than three days. When it was all over, Buddhist monks held a seven-day prayer chant for the souls of the dead birds.

As horrendous as the slaughter was, world influenza experts agreed that it probably prevented a bird flu pandemic. A few weeks later, virologist Yoshihiro Kawaoka, working at the University of Wisconsin, experimented with H5N1 in mice. He discovered the virus virtually dissolved mouse lungs and that it reproduced in other organs as well. "This is the most pathogenic virus that we know of," he said. "One infectious particle—one single infectious virus—kills mice." What will it do to humans? No one knows all the answers yet. H5N1. Remember it!

A team of Chinese public health workers wearing protective clothing set out to slaughter birds sold as food on December 30, 1997. The difficult but necessary measure helps prevent the spread of avian flu.

BLAME THE VIRUS, NOT THE BIRDS

Migratory waterfowl have carried flu viruses for thousands of years. Those birds are well adapted to flu viruses, and they seldom get sick. However, their droppings are highly infectious to domesticated birds, which have little immunity to flu viruses. A gram of infected bird droppings—less than one-quarter teaspoon—can sicken a million domesticated birds. Under cool weather conditions, the virus can survive for three months in bird droppings and for at least thirty days in water. Birds that get sick but survive bird flu, shed infectious viruses in their droppings and nasal secretions for at least ten days.

H5N1 is not the only kind of bird flu. Scientists have identified fifteen subtypes of bird flu. Over the past few years, several of these subtypes have changed in disturbing ways. First, the viruses are getting more deadly when they strike domesticated birds. A virus starts out just making chickens sick. Then within a few months, it becomes highly pathogenic, or more deadly. This process, called passage, was discussed in chapter 2. With each passage through the host species, a virus can become a more efficient killer.

For example, in 1983 an epidemic of the bird flu strain known as H5N2 struck chicken farms in Pennsylvania. At first, it killed only a few chickens. By the time the epidemic ended in 1984, H5N2 killed 9 out of 10 chickens it infected. Nearly every chicken in the state—more than 17 million birds—were culled, or destroyed, to halt that epidemic. In 1999 the same thing happened in Italy when another type of bird flu—H7N1—resulted in the death of 13 million chickens.

H5N1 is not the only bird flu virus to jump directly from birds to humans. The second worrisome change in bird flu viruses is that several varieties have developed this ability. None of the following bird flu viruses had ever been identified in humans before 1997. At least six strains have now been confirmed in people:

- 1997: H5N1 in Hong Kong
- 1999: H9N2 in Hong Kong
- 2002: H7N2 in Virginia
- 2003: H7N7 in the Netherlands
- 2004: H7N3 in Canada
- 2004: H10N7 in Egypt

By March 1, 2006, H5N1 bird flu had been found among wild birds, domestic birds, or animals in about 30 countries in Asia, Africa (Nigeria), the Middle East (Egypt and Iraq), and Europe (Austria, Germany, and Romania). Human cases have been confirmed in Cambodia, China, India, Indonesia, Iraq, Thailand, Turkey, and Vietnam. Most cases and most deaths have occurred in Indonesia, Thailand, and Vietnam. The virus has become endemic, that is constantly present, among wild and domesticated birds in Southeast Asia. Bird flu reached Nigeria early in 2006. By the middle of February 2006, wild migrating swans had carried it to Germany, Greece, and Italy. Experts believe migrating wild waterfowl and transport of infected poultry will carry the virus into the rest of Europe and more of Africa in the near future. No one can say when or if the virus will reach North and South America. Many people believe it is only a matter of time.

The outbreak of H7N7 in the Netherlands was huge, but largely overlooked in world news because SARS (sudden acute respiratory syndrome) broke out at the same time. Over 30 million birds and pigs were killed to stop the spread of H7N7. However, H5N1 remains by far the worst threat to humans of any of the bird viruses. It's the one people usually mean when they speak of bird flu.

Scientists are also concerned because H5N1 is showing up in unusual places. It's been found in bird species other than waterfowl, such as pigeons, sparrows, and eagles. It killed rare civets at a national park in Vietnam. It sickened tigers and leopards in Thailand zoos. During 2004, 147 captive tigers out of a population of 418 developed high fever and pneumonia. Until then, tigers were believed to be immune to Type A flu (which includes bird flu). The animals got sick after they'd devoured chicken carcasses from a farm known to have sick birds.

H5N1 has turned up in mammals other than pigs and tigers. Pet cats in Thai households were found to be infected. Laboratory researchers proved that domestic cats can not only get bird flu but spread it among themselves. Lab mice can also be infected experimentally with bird flu. The more species that H5N1 can infect, the greater the chance of a human pandemic.

The only thing that has delayed a probable pandemic of bird flu so far is that H5N1 does not readily pass between people. That could change at any time if H5N1 meets up with another flu virus while inside the body of a human or animal host. If the two viruses trade off genes, it could result in antigenic shift. If that happens—or when it happens as experts believe—the newly mutated virus could spread around the world in weeks, much like the less deadly SARS virus did.

Doctors are getting some nasty surprises when they care for patients with bird flu. Many patients have the usual flu symptoms of fever, cough, muscle aches, and sore throat. Others also get eye infections and viral pneumonia. Bacterial pneumonia is a complication that can follow influenza. It's less common for the flu virus itself to cause pneumonia. On autopsy, doctors sometimes find that the virus damages not just the respiratory system but the nervous and digestive systems, the heart, kidneys, and liver as well.

In 2005 doctors in Vietnam were shocked to discover that a young brother and sister who had died of severe diarrhea and encephalitis some months before had actually been infected with H5N1. Despite contact with sick birds, the children had never experienced breathing problems or any of the usual avian flu symptoms before they'd died. This alerted doctors to the possibility that people infected with H5N1 may display a variety of symptoms not seen before.

One thing bird flu seems to share with the 1918–1919 Spanish flu pandemic is that it hits young people especially hard. Many of the people who have developed bird flu have been children, teens, and young adults. These young people are dying of severe respiratory complications and multiple organ failure. It's normally the very young and the very old who are hardest hit by infectious diseases like flu. Nine out of ten of the people in the United States who die from the current flu strains are sixty-five years old or older.

Doctors are not sure why bird flu seems to target healthy children and young adults. It's possible those are the people who have most contact with sick poultry. Also, as with the Spanish flu, the immune response to bird flu in young people can be so extreme that it damages the body as much as the virus does.

MAKING PLANS

By early 2006, the world was on high alert, watching out for a bird flu pandemic. Experts estimate such a pandemic could kill tens of millions of people and sicken up to a third of the world's population as it did in 1918. The CDC, WHO, and health officials in every nation were scrambling to put plans in place to manage a pandemic when and if it comes. Scientists believe three conditions must be present in order for a flu pandemic to start:

- A new subtype of virus must emerge to which the general population has little or no immunity. H5N1 is that virus.

- The new virus must be able to reproduce inside humans and cause serious illness. H5N1 is that virus.

- The new virus must be easily transmitted between people. So far, H5N1 has been suspected of person-to-person contact in only a few cases. This is the step that researchers hope never happens.

In September 2005, Dr. Lee Jong-wook, director-general of the WHO said, "The virus is moving toward becoming transmissible by humans and the international community has no time to waste to prevent an epidemic." In November 2005, at another international WHO conference, he said, "It is only a matter of time before an avian flu virus—most likely H5N1—acquires the ability to be transmitted from human to human, sparking the outbreak of human pandemic influenza. We don't know when this will happen. But we do know that it will happen." The world is preparing for a possible bird flu pandemic in several ways.

Surveillance. Every human case of suspected bird flu is tracked. Some of the questions to be answered are these: Where did the infection come from? Did other family members get ill? Did health-care workers who took care of the sick people get sick themselves? Does it seem that person-to-person transmission occurred? What is the range of symptoms experienced? Most important of all, do laboratory tests confirm that the disease is H5N1?

Government officials around the world are now monitoring and testing sick birds. In the United States, Alaskan birds are heavily tested because many migratory birds enter by that route. Most states are also testing their poultry flocks on a regular basis.

China alone is home to *13 billion* chickens, most raised in small flocks on rural family farms. People get sick with bird flu when they work around sick chickens or when they prepare them to eat (thoroughly cooking chicken meat kills the viruses). People have also developed bird flu after eating a type of soup made with raw blood from infected ducks. All sick birds and birds in contact with them must be culled. This devastates families who depend on their birds for both income and food. After the culling, farms and equipment must be disinfected to kill lingering viruses.

Quarantine and travel restrictions. Quarantine—the practice of keeping sick people isolated from others—has

Quarantined students look out a window at a Chinese university during the 2003 SARS outbreak in that country.

been practiced for centuries. In 2003 the strict quarantine of patients in hospitals and of families in their homes helped to contain the SARS outbreak. The flu is more contagious than SARS was, and bird flu is much more lethal than SARS.

During a speech in October 2005, President Bush said military force might be used to enforce a quarantine. In 2006 the CDC announced the U.S. government has the right to isolate or quarantine sick people traveling into the country, especially if they have a respiratory illness that might be bird flu. State and local health authorities are in charge of the quarantine plans for their own citizens. This could include shutting down schools, workplaces, stores, movie theaters, and churches.

It could take just a few weeks for bird flu to make its way around the world because people do so much traveling. In 2000 more than 18 million commercial airline flights took off from global airports, carrying 1.1 billion passengers. Millions more traveled by car, bus, ship, and train. Health officials talk about the possible need for quarantine in the event of a widespread bird flu outbreak. Such a quarantine could temporarily halt or delay travel in many parts of the world.

Vaccine. Effective flu vaccines have been in use for decades. However, bird flu is so deadly to chickens that the time-tested method of using fertile eggs to make the vaccine cannot be used. When scientists tried to develop a vaccine after the first cases of bird flu in 1997, they discovered that the virus killed the chicken embryos long before the vaccine was ready. It took a year of genetic engineering of the virus to make it possible to grow it inside eggs only to discover in 2004 that the virus had mutated so much, researchers had to scrap everything and start all over again.

Small amounts of an experimental H5N1 vaccine began limited testing in 2005 in the United States. Early results proved promising. Based on the vaccine's effectiveness to induce antibodies against H5N1, the U.S. government ordered several million doses to be stored in the event of an outbreak of bird flu. However, if H5N1 becomes a pandemic, it's possible the newly mutated virus could not be prevented by current experimental vaccines. Also, in order for a vaccine against a totally new flu such as H5N1 to be effective, people must receive two injections a few weeks apart to build up immunity. It could be catastrophic if a pandemic of H5N1 broke out before a working vaccine was developed. No one has any natural immunity to the virus, so ideally, all *6.5 billion* people on the planet should be vaccinated.

Antiviral medications. In the face of a possible bird flu pandemic for which there is not yet an effective vaccine, some nations are stockpiling antiviral medications. Only the neuraminidase inhibitors Tamiflu and Relenza are believed useful in helping to prevent or treat bird flu. However, these medications are very expensive and are generally available only to citizens of wealthier countries. They are in chronic short supply in any event. Additionally, all flu viruses tend to become resistant to antiviral medications.

Still, WHO believes neuraminidase inhibitors will be especially important if a bird flu pandemic breaks out before a vaccine is widely available. (Yet some researchers say that these medications will have little or no affect during a bird flu pandemic.) The medications can be given to health-care workers and exposed family members to help prevent bird flu. If sick people are identified early enough—within the first forty-eight hours—the medications can be given to decrease the severity of their illness.

STAGES OF A PANDEMIC

The World Health Organization defines the stages of an influenza pandemic in its Global Influenza Preparedness Plan. As of early spring 2006, WHO and the CDC said the world was at stage 3. The stages are:

The Interpandemic Period

Phase 1: No new influenza virus subtypes have been detected in humans. An influenza virus subtype that has caused human infection may be present in animals. If present in animals, the risk of human infection or disease is considered to be low.

Phase 2: No new influenza virus subtypes have been detected in humans. However, a circulating animal influenza virus subtype poses a substantial risk of human disease.

Pandemic Alert Period

Phase 3: Human infection(s) with a new subtype but no human-to-human spread, or at most rare instances of spread to a close contact.

Phase 4: Small cluster(s) with limited human-to-human transmission, but spread is highly localized, suggesting that the virus is not well adapted to humans.

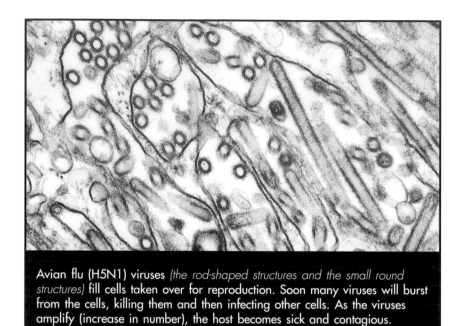

Avian flu (H5N1) viruses *(the rod-shaped structures and the small round structures)* fill cells taken over for reproduction. Soon many viruses will burst from the cells, killing them and then infecting other cells. As the viruses amplify (increase in number), the host becomes sick and contagious.

Phase 5: Larger cluster(s) but human-to-human spread still localized, suggesting that the virus is becoming increasingly better adapted to humans but may not yet be fully transmissible (substantial pandemic risk).

Pandemic Period

Phase 6: Pandemic: increased and sustained transmission in general population.

Even before bird flu appeared in humans in 1997, scientists recognized the fact that the world is overdue for another influenza pandemic. Around the world in private laboratories and government research facilities, investigators are looking for newer and better ways to identify, prevent, and treat all strains of flu. Read about some of them in the next chapter.

PANDEMIC FLU PLANNING CHECKLIST

Talk to your family about preparing a plan for the possibility of pandemic flu. Some experts say every family should be prepared to stay in their home and take care of themselves for six to eight weeks. The actions you take can lessen the impact of an influenza pandemic on you and your family. You can store supplies in large plastic storage bins and keep them in a closet or basement.

1. To plan for a pandemic:

- Gather a supply of water and food. During a pandemic, if you cannot get to a store or if stores are closed or out of food, it will be important to have extra supplies on hand. This can be useful in other emergencies, such as power outages and natural disasters.

- Family members should keep an extra supply of their regular prescription drugs.

- Have nonprescription drugs and other health supplies on hand, including pain relievers, stomach remedies, cough and cold medicines, vitamins, and fluids with electrolytes (sports drinks and infant drinks such as Pedialyte).

- Consider keeping some cash in the house, and be sure every family member knows where it is.

- Make a contact list with the name, phone numbers, and addresses of other family members, close friends, and emergency organizations.
- Volunteer with local community groups to prepare for an influenza pandemic.

2. To limit the spread of germs and prevent infection:

- Be sure everyone in your family washes their hands with soap and water correctly and frequently.
- Always cover coughs and sneezes with tissues.
- Stay away from sick people as much as possible.
- People who are sick should stay home from work and school.

3. Items to have on hand for an extended stay at home:

- Food and nonperishable supplies

    Bottled water (allow for one gallon per person per day)

    Ready-to-eat canned meats, fruits, vegetables, chili, and soups

    Protein, granola, or fruit bars

    Dry cereal or granola

    Peanut butter or nuts

    Dried fruit

Crackers

Fruit juices in boxes or cans

Cans or jars of baby food
and formula

Pet food

- Medical, health, and emergency supplies

Medical supplies such as diabetic
and blood pressure monitors

First aid kit (the bigger, the better)

First aid book

Soap and alcohol-based hand
washes

Fever medicines such as ibuprofen
or acetaminophen

Thermometer

Household cleaners and disinfectants

Disposable dishes, glasses, and eating utensils (paper and plastic)

Flashlight and batteries

Candles and matches

Battery-operated radio or television

Manual can opener

Garbage bags

Paper products such as tissues,
toilet paper, and disposable diapers
for infants and toddlers

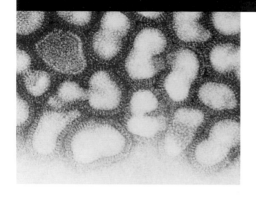

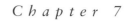

Chapter 7

FLU RESEARCH

Much of today's research is focused on finding better ways to make and use flu vaccines. During the vaccine shortages of the 2004–2005 flu season, doctors first experimented with giving smaller doses to healthy people. They used one-fifth of the usual amount and gave it under the skin with a short needle instead of giving it into the muscle with a longer needle. The surprising results showed a vigorous antibody response in people eighteen to sixty years old, but not among people older than sixty. This means that the supply of flu vaccine could protect many more people than previously realized.

Researchers are working on ways to produce flu vaccine without eggs. One way is to grow the viruses in monkey or dog cells or to use human stem cells. So far, success has been limited. One experimental vaccine caused more side effects than expected, and testing was postponed. A slightly different approach to producing a vaccine uses tiny beads called microcarriers covered with monkey kidney cells. It's hoped that flu viruses will grow well on microcarriers, but testing a vaccine made this way is a long way off. In another series of experiments, a baculovirus (a virus that preys on insects, which is not harmful to humans) is genetically combined with the flu virus and inserted into caterpillar cells. The infected cells produce a substance which can be purified and used to make a flu vaccine. A vaccine made by this method was undergoing clinical testing in humans in early 2006. Flu proteins might even be grown in potatoes or bananas! If these methods prove successful, vaccines can be produced faster and people with egg allergies will be able to take them.

Nations around the world are working hard to develop a safe and effective bird flu vaccine. In 2004 the U.S. government ordered two million doses of bird flu vaccine, even before it had been developed. The first testing of a bird flu vaccine on healthy adult volunteers began in the spring of 2005. U.S. scientists are also working on a vaccine for another kind of bird flu—H9N2. Although it's less deadly than H5N1, it has killed people and resulted in the death of millions of birds.

China vaccinated about *2.7 billion* ducks, chickens, and geese against bird flu in fourteen months. (An estimated 5.2

Workers in Asia vaccinate chickens against the bird flu in 2005 as part of an international effort to stop transmission of the illness from birds to humans.

billion chickens and other poultry live in China.) In 2006 China announced the development of a new vaccine for its poultry. Instead of having to inject each bird individually, the new vaccine can be sprayed over flocks of birds. This method is cheaper and faster, making it an attractive alternative for poorer nations. While it's impossible to vaccinate all birds, vaccinating many of the chickens living in small Asian farms could help to break the chain of bird-to-bird and bird-to-human transmission.

FAR-OUT RESEARCH

Vaccines aren't the only area of flu research. Scientists wonder why bird flu hasn't infected more people yet or why it seems difficult to pass between people. They believe that H5N1 must mix genes with a human flu virus in order to become more contagious. Rather than waiting to see if nature spawns such a hybrid on its own, CDC scientists are going to do it themselves. Deep inside its most secure

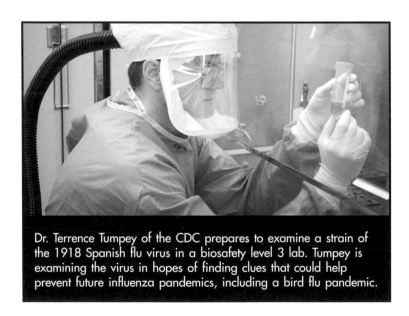

Dr. Terrence Tumpey of the CDC prepares to examine a strain of the 1918 Spanish flu virus in a biosafety level 3 lab. Tumpey is examining the virus in hopes of finding clues that could help prevent future influenza pandemics, including a bird flu pandemic.

biosafety level 3 facility, the CDC is experimenting on combining H5N1 with H3N2, the flu strain circulating today. If successful, the new strain would be tested on animals to determine how contagious or lethal it might be. This dangerous yet important work could give the world a head start in knowing how a natural genetic mutation might occur. Other areas of study include:

- The National Institute of Allergy and Infectious Diseases (NIAID) is leading a project to complete genetic sequencing of all flu strains.

- NIAID is funding research into using human flu antibodies in a powdered nasal spray to boost the immune system. It has already worked successfully in mice.

- NIAID is funding research into a do-it-yourself flu vaccination kit. Instead of a scary-looking syringe, the device looks like a ballpoint pen and has a retractable needle. Once filled with vaccine, it could be mailed to millions of people who cannot readily reach a doctor's office or clinic. It would be as easy to use as the gadget that diabetics use to test their blood sugar.

- Public and private researchers are working on small devices nicknamed labs-on-a-chip to quickly detect and identify flu viruses. These genetic-based tests would be far more accurate than the tests used to diagnose flu today.

MAKING PLANS

The U.S. government released its first national pandemic influenza plan in 1978, shortly after swine flu created worries of an outbreak of a new flu strain. The U.S. Department of Health and Human Services released its newest version in November 2005. It's likely to be updated at least yearly.

Officials attend an international WHO meeting in 2006 to strategize plans for dealing with the bird flu. The meeting is part of WHO's ongoing effort to stave off a bird flu pandemic.

Among its goals are the implementation of public health measures to limit the spread of infection by isolation and quarantine as needed, and the administration of stockpiled antiviral medications and vaccine (if available) to priority groups such as health-care workers and first responders.

The plan stresses the importance of surveillance, the need for additional vaccine research, the necessity to vaccinate at-risk populations, and the stockpiling of antiviral medications. It proposes methods to stop the spread of flu should a pandemic develop. As of 2006, world health authorities say we've moved out of what had been called the "interpandemic period," and we are now in the "pandemic alert period."

In November of 2004, WHO scheduled an international meeting in Geneva, Switzerland, to discuss the need for ongoing research into vaccines. Representatives from the United States, Europe, Japan, Russia, Australia, and other industrialized nations attended as did nearly every flu vaccine manufacturer in the world. The need to develop flu vaccines without using fertile chicken eggs was stressed. Under the current process, about 300 million doses of flu vaccine are made each year, only a fraction of what is needed to vaccinate the world's population.

The World Health Organization continues to update its influenza pandemic preparedness plan, originally published in 1999. A report published by WHO in 2005 expressed concern about "the general lack of preparedness for an influenza pandemic." It also pointed out that H5N1 may be "evolving in ways that increasingly favor the start of a pandemic" because the virus is becoming more lethal to birds, it's hardier and living longer in the environment, and it has expanded its range of mammal hosts. Lastly, the report states that the present situation regarding H5N1 in some ways resembles the 1918–1919 pandemic in that the virus causes severe disease, it strikes people who are younger and healthier, and humans have no immunity to it.

WHOM TO PROTECT?

The shortage of flu vaccine during the 2004–2005 flu season forced health officials to limit vaccinations for the first time. Only the most needy, such as people over sixty-five years old, health-care workers with direct patient contact, children between six and twenty-four months, and those with chronic medical conditions could be vaccinated. Images of old people waiting in line for hours to get their shots filled the news. Healthy adults between fifty and sixty-four who normally get vaccinated were turned down, as were healthy people of most ages. Yet some vaccine ended up going to waste when many people who should have received a flu shot stayed away because they believed they should save the vaccine for people sicker than themselves.

The vaccine shortage started health officials thinking about whom to protect and how to best protect them. In the United States, flu vaccine is used to reduce illness and death in susceptible populations. Current medical ethics mandate first protecting those most at risk for severe illness or death. That makes sense. Society doesn't want to see people die unnecessarily.

However, the practice of vaccinating the sick and elderly doesn't keep flu from spreading. In order to control an epidemic, healthy young people who are highly mobile and in contact with many other people are the ones who must be vaccinated. That includes children, teens, college students, working adults, and especially health-care workers. Unless one of the experimental methods of producing vaccine is perfected, it's almost certain that there will not be enough vaccine to protect everyone during a flu pandemic.

Will it be more important to protect people who might die from the flu? Or will it be more important to protect the younger, healthier population who spread it? If at-risk people are not protected, many would surely die who might have been saved. If the younger population is not protected, millions would get sick and entire economies might shut down—at least temporarily. That happened with the Spanish flu, and it took a decade for the world to recover.

That's not the only question medical ethicists wrestle with. During a pandemic, should people be forced to get a flu vaccination even if they don't want one? Similar measures are in place for tuberculosis. Laws in many states require people with tuberculosis to accept treatment. They can even be arrested if they refuse to complete their treatment. During a flu pandemic, should sick people be quarantined at home or in hospitals? That helped stop the spread of SARS in 2003, and President Bush said he would use the military for this purpose if necessary. An individual's right to refuse treatment versus the rights of the public to be protected against infectious disease is always a matter for heated debate.

Dozens of new diseases have moved from animals to humans over the past fifty years as a growing world population takes over animal habitats. In addition to bird flu, some of the most widely known are:

- HIV/AIDS (may have reached people when they ate infected African chimps)
- SARS (from small mammals sold as food in Asian markets)
- hantavirus and Lassa fever (carried by rodents)
- Lyme disease (from ticks)
- human monkeypox (from monkeys)
- mad cow disease (started in Great Britain by feeding contaminated bonemeal and protein supplements made from diseased animals to cattle, causes deadly brain wasting in cattle and humans)

It almost seems as if nature itself is a bioterrorist. Yet we have conquered many infectious diseases. In 1977 WHO declared the world free of smallpox (except some samples kept for research). In most countries, children no longer get diphtheria, polio, measles, mumps, or tetanus. SARS was identified and contained by global health authorities in just one hundred days! That quick victory showed it's possible to control outbreaks of infectious diseases when the world's countries work together.

In 2005 Dr. Lee Jong-wook, director-general of the World Health Organization, said in a report about bird flu, "The H5N1 virus has given us not only a clear warning, but time to enhance preparedness." His words offer hope that we still have not yet run out of time. Compared to the flu pandemics of the twentieth century, mankind can prepare for the next flu pandemic, whether it's bird flu or another strain yet to be identified.

ALTERNATIVE OPINIONS

Not everyone agrees that avian influenza H5N1 will become the next pandemic. Some researchers believe the virus may not necessarily mutate into a form that will make it more transmissible among humans. Others believe that H5N1 occurs much more often in people than has been recognized. World health authorities only know about possible or confirmed cases of H5N1 if local hospitals and doctors report them. Perhaps many people get bird flu and suffer only a mild illness, never needing to seek medical care.

Some people point to the Y2K experience. Most computers had not been programmed to recognize a year beginning with anything other than 19. It was believed that the world's computers would crash on December 31, 1999, because they couldn't "read" the year 2000. People stored food, supplies, and money in their homes in the belief that society would suffer an economic collapse. Of course, this did not happen.

Perhaps no other disease has been more closely watched from the beginning than H5N1. Whatever happens, bird flu cannot sneak up on us. Every known case in the world is monitored, counted, and followed to its conclusion. We can keep ourselves well informed by visiting reputable websites and reading reliable media reports. Unlike people living in 1918, we have time to prepare for a possible pandemic.

GLOSSARY

antibiotics: medications used to fight infections caused by bacteria and some parasites (such as malaria); antibiotics do not kill viruses.

antibodies: proteins produced in the body as an immune response to help defend against invading foreign substances, such as viruses and bacteria

antigen: substances that cause the body to produce antibodies in an allergic or immune response; they include proteins such as those found in viruses, bacteria, pollen, and foods.

antigen drift: the gradual but continual mutation that flu viruses undergo; these changes are the reason new flu vaccines must be formulated each year.

antigen shift: sudden changes in the hemagglutinin or neuraminidase of a Type A flu virus, which results in a new subtype of the virus. These changes are so significant that they may cause pandemics because people have little or no natural resistance to them.

antiviral medications: medications used to fight infections caused by viruses

asthma: a disease in which the tiny airways inside the lungs spasm and constrict, making it difficult to breathe.

avian flu: the H5N1 strain of bird flu has only been known to infect man since 1997. It's highly lethal to a wide variety of birds, and it kills about half of the people who get it.

Centers for Disease Control and Prevention (CDC): the U.S. federal agency responsible for monitoring and tracking diseases. Among other activities, the CDC is charged with protecting the health and safety of Americans.

cull: to select, gather, or choose; in this book, *culling* refers to collecting and killing sick or exposed birds.

culture: the process of growing a microorganism, such as a bacteria or virus, in a specially prepared nutrient medium or living cell

DNA (deoxyribonucleic acid): genetic material found in all living organisms and many viruses

emphysema: a lung condition where permanent damage occurs to the airways and alveoli (tiny air sacs deep inside the lungs); most often caused by smoking

endemic: a disease commonly present most of the time in a limited region; bird flu, for example, is endemic to domesticated fowl of Southeast Asia.

epidemic: a disease outbreak over a wide geographical area; for example, over the past few years, there have been epidemics of measles in countries of the former Soviet Union.

gene: segments of DNA or RNA that contain the information that determines how an organism will live and reproduce

Guillain-Barré syndrome: a rare neurological disorder that sometimes follows the flu; a temporary paralysis begins in the legs and moves up the body.

Haemophilus influenzae: the bacteria once mistakenly believed to cause influenza

hemagglutinin: one of two protein protuberances of a flu virus, hemagglutinin allows the virus to attach to and invade host cells.

H5N1: the Type A strain flu virus that causes bird flu

inoculation: the introduction of a substance into a body; most often used to mean vaccination

mutation: a random and natural mistake occurring during genetic replication that may result in a defect being passed to future generations of an organism. Most mutations are harmful; however, some may help the organism adapt to a changing environment.

neuraminidase: one of two kinds of protein protuberances of a flu virus, neuraminidase allows the virus to move among cells in order to spread the infection.

pandemic: an outbreak of disease that has spread around the world; for example, the 1918–1919 Spanish flu pandemic

passage: the process of a virus moving from one host to another; with each passage, the virus may change and become more lethal.

quarantine: the act of isolating people who have infectious diseases in a hospital or in their homes so they cannot spread the infection to others

Reye's syndrome: a rare and potentially fatal disorder of the brain and liver that can develop in people, especially children, after taking aspirin for viral infections

RNA (ribonucleic acid): genetic material in some viruses (such as influenza viruses) that directs protein synthesis and replication

Severe Acute Respiratory Syndrome (SARS): the new disease that broke out in 2003 for the first time; caused by a virus related to a common cold virus

surveillance: the systematic collection and analysis of information about diseases usually conducted by governmental health organizations, such as the CDC and WHO

vaccination: the process of injecting (usually) a dead or weakened bacteria or virus in order to stimulate the immune system to form antibodies against disease

vaccine: the substance used for vaccination. Most vaccines are injectable liquids; a nasal spray flu vaccine is available, and the polio vaccine is oral.

virus: tiny infectious particles that require a living host (a plant or animal cell) to survive and reproduce

World Health Organization (WHO): an international organization that's part of the United Nations. Its goal is to improve the health of people around the world.

RESOURCES

Information about flu can be found through an Internet search using the following key words: "influenza," "flu," "bird flu," or "avian flu." You also can get information by calling or writing the following organizations or by reviewing their online websites:

Centers for Disease Control and Prevention (CDC)
1600 Clifton Road
Atlanta, GA 30333
(800) 311-3435
http://www.cdc.gov

The CDC's mission is to promote health and quality of life by preventing and controlling disease, injury, and disability. The CDC conducts disease research to develop methods to better identify, control, and cure diseases. It also monitors and investigates health problems around the world and in the United States. Each week it releases its Morbidity and Mortality Weekly Report (http://www.cdc.gov/mmwr), which tracks many health-related issues, as well as disease outbreaks. For information about influenza, go directly to http://www.cdc.gov/flu.

Infectious Diseases Society of America
66 Canal Center Plaza, Suite 600
Alexandria, VA 22314
(703) 299-0200
http://www.idsociety.org

This organization of doctors, scientists, and other health-care professionals specializes in infectious diseases. Its goals are to improve the health of individuals, communities, and society by promoting excellence in patient care, education, research, public health, and prevention relating to infectious diseases. While the website is intended primarily for health-care workers, it contains much information on a variety of topics.

MedlinePlus
Sponsored by: U.S. National Library of Medicine and the National Institutes of Health
http://www.nlm.nih.gov/medlineplus/flu.html

103

An ever-changing and frequently updated collection of articles about influenza, including information about prevention, symptoms, diagnosis, treatment, and many links to articles from reputable public service and governmental health organizations.

National Institute of Allergy and Infectious Diseases (NIAID)
Office of Communications & Public Liaison
6610 Rockledge Drive, MSC 6612
Bethesda, MD 20892
(301) 496-5717
http://www.niaid.nih.gov

Part of the National Institutes of Health, NIAID conducts and supports research to better understand, treat, and prevent infectious, immunologic, and allergic diseases. Its work has contributed to new testing methods, treatments, and vaccines that have improved the health of millions of people in the United States and around the world. For information about influenza go to http://www.niaid.nih.gov/dmid/influenza.

World Health Organization (WHO)
Avenue Appia 20
1211 Geneva 27, Switzerland
(41 22) 791 2111
http://www.who.int/en

WHO is part of the United Nations. Its objective is the attainment by all people of the highest possible level of health. The organization defines health not merely as the absence of disease but as a state of complete physical, mental, and social well-being. The website offers updated information about disease outbreaks around the world. For information specific to influenza, go to http://www.who.int/topics/influenza/en.

FURTHER READING

Barry, J. M. *The Great Influenza: The Epic Story of the Deadliest Plague in History*. New York: Viking, 2004. (Adult book about the Spanish flu pandemic)

Davis, Mike. *The Monster at Our Door: The Global Threat of Avian Flu*. New York: New Press, 2005. (Young adult book about the growing threat of an avian flu pandemic)

Drexler, Madeline. *Secret Agents: The Menace of Emerging Infections*. New York: Penguin Books, 2003. (Adult book about many infectious diseases, including influenza)

Fridell, Ron. *Decoding Life: Unraveling the Mysteries of the Genome*. Minneapolis: Lerner Publications Company, 2004. (Young adult book about the Human Genome Project, genetics, and more)

Friedlander, Mark P. *Outbreak: Disease Detectives at Work*. Minneapolis, Lerner Publications Company, 2000. (Young adult introduction to the field of epidemiology, it's history, and case studies)

Getz, David. *Purple Death*. New York: Henry Holt, 2000. (Young adult book about the Spanish flu pandemic)

Goldsmith, Connie. *Invisible Invaders: Dangerous Infectious Diseases*. Minneapolis: Twenty-First Century Books, 2006. (Young adult book about emerging and reemerging infectious diseases, including bird flu)

Preston, Richard. *The Demon in the Freezer*. New York: Random House, 2002. (Easy-to-read adult book about the study and use of stored smallpox strains and their implications)

———. *The Hot Zone*. Rockland, MA: Wheeler Publishing, 1995. (Easy-to-read adult book about the study and spread of the deadly Ebola and Marburg viruses and their pandemic potential)

Ramen, Fred. *Epidemics—Deadly Diseases Throughout History: Influenza*. New York: Rosen, 2001. (Young adult book about influenza)

SOURCE NOTES

19   Madeline Drexler, *Secret Agents: The Menace of Emerging Infections* (New York: Penguin Books, 2003), 164.

30   N. R. Grist, "Pandemic Influenza 1918." *British Medical Journal,* (December 22–29, 1979), 1632–1633.

78   Drexler, 180.

95   WHO, *Influenza Pandemic Preparedness and Response: Report by the Secretariat,* 2005, http://www.who.int/gb/ebwha/pdf_files/EB115/B115_44-en.pdf (January 2006).

95   WHO, *Avian Influenza: Assessing the Pandemic Threat,* 2005, http://www.who.int/csr/disease/influenza/H5N1-9reduit.pdf (January 2006).

SELECTED BIBLIOGRAPHY

Barry, J. M. *The Great Influenza: The Epic Story of the Deadliest Plague in History.* New York: Viking, 2004.

Belshe, R. B., et al. "Serum Antibody Responses after Intradermal Vaccination against influenza." *The New England Journal of Medicine*, (2004), 2,286–2,294.

CDC. "CDC Announces Change in Recommendations for Use of Antivirals; Clinicians Should Not Prescribe Two Common Antivirals." *CDC.* January 14, 2006. http://www.cdc.gov/od/oc/media/pressrel/r060114.htm (January 2006).

———. "Weekly Report: Influenza Summary Update, Week ending January 7, 2006—Week 1." *CDC: Influenza (Flu).* N.d. http://www.cdc.gov/flu/weekly/weeklyarchives2005-2006/weekly01.htm (February 2006).

Drexler, Madeline. *Secret Agents: The Menace of Emerging Infections.* New York: Penguin Books, 2003.

Friedlander, M. P., and T. M. Phillips. *The Immune System: Your Body's Disease-Fighting Army.* Minneapolis: Lerner Publications Company, 1998.

Getz, David. *Purple Death.* New York: Henry Holt, 2000.

Grist, N. R. "Pandemic Influenza 1918." *British Medical Journal*, December 22–29, 1979, 1,632–1,633.

Heymann, D. L., ed. *Control of Communicable Diseases Manual.* 18th ed. Washington, DC: American Public Health Association, 2004.

Jefferson, T., et al. "Antivirals for Influenza in Healthy Adults: Systemic Review," *The Lancet*, 2006, 303–313.

Keawcharoen J., et al. "Avian Influenza H5N1 in Tigers and Leopards." *Emerging Infectious Diseases*, 2004, 2189–2191.

Kolata, Gina. *Flu: The Story of the Great Influenza Pandemic of 1918.* New York: Farrar, Straus and Giroux, 1999.

Marchione, M. Associated Press. "Flu-Shot Supply Tough to Hurry." *Sacramento Bee*, October 24, 2004.

Marshall, Mike. "1918 Spanish Flu Paralyzed the City." *Huntsville Times*. 2005. http://www.al.com/news/huntsvilletimes/index.ssf?/base/news/1114334498292321.xml (February 2006).

McCain, J. "Health Plans Respond as Microbes Develop Resistance Techniques." *Managed Care Magazine.* 2003. http://www.managedcaremag.com/archives/0406/0406.antibiotics .html (February 2006).

Nourse, Alan E. *The Virus Invaders.* New York: Franklin Watts, 1992.

Perlin, D., and A. Cohen. *The Complete Idiot's Guide to Dangerous Diseases and Epidemics.* Indianapolis: Alpha/Pearson, 2002.

Ramen, Fred. *Epidemics—Deadly Diseases throughout History: Influenza.* New York: Rosen, 2001.

Schull, P. D. *Nursing Spectrum Drug Handbook.* King of Prussia, PA: MedVantage Publishing, 2005.

Smolinski, M. S., et al. *Microbial Threats to Health.* Washington, DC: Institute of Medicine's National Academies Press, 2003.

Taubenberger, J. K. "1918 Influenza: The Mother of All Pandemics." *Emerging Infectious Diseases,* 2006, 15–22.

Thompson, W. W., et al. "Influenza-Associated Hospitalizations in the United States." *Journal of the American Medical Association,* 2004, 1,333–1,340.

Treanor, J. "Weathering the Influenza Vaccine Crisis." *The New England Journal of Medicine,* 2004, 2,037–2,040.

INDEX

AIDS/HIV, 11, 13, 35, 97
antibodies, 36, 52, 53, 55, 65,
  69, 84, 93, 99
antigen, 14, 16, 20, 74, 99
antigenic drift, 17, 18, 33, 37, 99
antigenic shift, 17, 37, 73, 80,
  84, 99
antiviral medication, 57, 63, 64,
  67 69, 71, 84–85, 94
avian flu. *See* bird flu

bacteria, 13, 22–23, 28, 44, 46,
  58, 60, 63, 67, 71, 99. *See
  also* pneumonia, bacterial;
  Black Plague, the; bubonic
  plague
bird flu, 10–11, 20, 71, 72–86
Black Plague, the, 10, 32. *See
  also* plague
bubonic plague, 22. *See also*
  plague

capsid, 13
Centers for Disease Control and
  Prevention (CDC), 55, 56, 63,
  64, 69, 70, 76, 81, 83, 85,
  92–93, 100
chicken pox. *See* diseases, virus-
  caused
China, 18, 19, 26, 37, 77, 79,
  82, 91
contagious, 11, 22, 42, 83, 86,
  92, 93

daughter virus. *See* virus,
  daughter
diagnosis, 63–66

diseases, virus-caused; chicken
  pox, 13, 50, 70; cholera, 51;
  diphtheria, 51, 97; Ebola, 14;
  hantavirus, 13, 97; Lassa
  fever, 97; measles, 18, 24, 28,
  47, 51, 97, 100; mumps, 18,
  50, 97, polio, 13, 18, 50, 97,
  102; smallpox, 22, 33, 50;
  tetanus, 51, 97; West Nile
  virus, 13; whooping cough,
  51; yellow fever, 14, 51. *See
  also* flu (influenza)
deoxyribonucleic acid (DNA), 13,
  100

envelope, 13; lipid, 16
epidemic, 9–11, 17, 21–38, 59,
  66, 78, 82, 96, 100. *See also*
  pandemic

fatty membrane, 13
fever: as diagnostic tool, 63;
  in animals, 79–80; as
  complication, 70, 71; as
  flu symptom, 9, 14, 37,
  40, 42, 44 45, 47, 73, 76;
  hemorrhafic, 14; three-day,
  26–27; treatment of, 66, 75,
  89; as vaccine side effect, 52,
  55, 57; yellow, 14, 51
flu (influenza): Asian, 37;
  complications, 9, 46–48, 69,
  71; Hong Kong, 37; immune
  system response, 44, 46,
  81–82, 93, 99; la grippe,
  (ordinary flu), 30; naming, 20,
  30; Russian, 22; season,

109

41–42; shot (vaccine), 18, 38, 50, 53–56, 62; stomach flu, 44; strains, 20, 53, 66, 74; swine, 38, 47, 93; tests, 64, 65, 66; treatment of, 62–71; Type A, 14, 19, 20, 37, 38, 54, 65, 68, 74, 80, 99, 101; Type B, 19–20, 54, 65, 68; Type C, 19–20; vaccine supply, chronology of, 58–59; virus, 14, 16–18, 19, 22–24, 27–29, 36, 37, 42–44, 46, 52, 66, 73–75, 78, 80, 82, 91, 92, 99, 101; in waterfowl, 19, 74, 78, 79. *See also* bird flu; Guillain-Barré syndrome; pigs
Food and Drug Administration (FDA), 57, 59, 70

genetics, 10; gene exchange, 11, 15; information in a virus, 13; material, 13; recombination of genes, 11, 15. *See also* deoxyribonucleic acid (DNA); mutate and mutation; ribonucleic acid (RNA)
Guillain-Barré syndrome, 38, 46–47, 100

hantavirus. *See* diseases, virus-caused
hemagglutinin, 16–17, 20, 43, 74, 99
Hong Kong, 37, 75, 76, 79
hospital and hospitalization, 9, 24, 27, 28, 29, 31, 40, 42, 63, 65, 73, 75, 76, 83, 96, 98, 101
host, 12, 13, 14, 16, 67–68, 78, 80, 86, 95, 101, 102

immune system, 14–17, 40–46, 52, 53, 55–57, 69, 102;

response to flu virus, 44, 46, 81–82, 93, 99
immunity, 37, 50, 52, 74, 78, 80, 81, 84, 95
immunization. *See* flu: shot (vaccine)
incubation period, 42
infectious 52, 78, 101; cloud, 43; diseases, 34, 47, 51, 66, 81, 93, 97, 102. *See also* diseases, virus-caused
influenza. *See* flu (influenza)
inoculation (vaccination), 50, 101

Jenner, William, 50, 51

Kawaoka, Yoshihiro, 77

la grippe (influenza). *See* flu (influenza)
lipids (fatty acids), 13

measles. *See* diseases, virus-caused
Miner, Loring, 24–25
mutate and mutation, 11, 15, 16, 17, 22, 27, 33, 53, 74, 80, 84, 98, 99, 101; genetic, 15, 74, 93

nasal: secretions, 78; spray, 57, 58, 59, 93, 102; swab, 76
national pandemic influenza plan, 93–94
neuraminidase, 16–17, 20, 68, 74, 84, 85, 99, 101

onset: of infection, 71; of symptoms, 42, 44, 45, 67
Orthomyxoviridae, 16

pandemic, 10, 14, 17, 20, 22, 23, 33–38, 71, 73, 74, 77,

ABOUT THE AUTHOR

Connie Goldsmith is a registered nurse with a bachelor of science degree in nursing and a master of public administration degree in health care. In addition to writing several nonfiction books for middle school and upper-grade readers, Goldsmith has also published more than two hundred magazine articles, mostly on health topics for adults and children. She writes a children's book review column for a regional parenting magazine in Sacramento, California, where she lives.